Deer Hunting

Tactics for Today's Big-Game Hunter

*To Jason —
Good Hunting!*

Gary Lewis

2012

by Gary Lewis

DEER HUNTING
Tactics for Today's Big-Game Hunter
Copyright © 2003 by Gary Lewis

ISBN 0971410062

Cover design by Dyan R. Roth, Bend, Oregon
Interior design by Katherine Lloyd, The DESK, Bend, Oregon
Cover photo by GaryKramer.net

Gary Lewis Outdoors
PO Box 1364
Bend, Oregon 97709
541-317-0116

Printed in the United States of America

Dedication

This book is dedicated to all men and women who call themselves
deer hunters, who love the pursuit of our North American deer,
these most beautiful and graceful of wild creatures.

Acknowledgements

Thank you to Ed Park for your contribution and for the help
along the way. *Thank you* to my wife Merrilee for your help.
Thank you Katherine Lloyd for your work with layout and editing.
Thank you to Dave Hamilton and
James Flaherty for your editing, but most of all
for your insight and friendship.

Thank You Lord for the order of Your creation
and for the interest You take in each of us.

The author with an eastern Oregon mule deer buck. Gary Lewis photo.

This Oregon blacktail was taken on the second day of the season in cover so thick and dry that no hunter could enter undetected. The one weakness to his hideout was that a corner of his bedroom could be seen from a nearby mountain. Gary Lewis photo.

TABLE OF CONTENTS

Eastern Oregon mule deer taken with a 7mm Magnum. Gary Lewis photo.

Foreword to Deer Hunting

by Wayne Van Zwoll

L ong ago, on the bank of Oregon's Willamette River, a blacktail buck jumped into a thicket before I could bring my rifle to bear. I circled the thicket downwind and sneaked into it, a baby-step at a time. Even now, that sparsely leafed, gray-brown screen of November blackberries, alders, and willows pops into mind as a place of drama. It was ideal deer cover, almost too thick to penetrate, far too noisy for a quiet stalk, the kind of cover I've often hunted poorly because I didn't have the patience to hunt it well.

But when you know there's a deer in the same place you are, hunting well becomes an imperative. So I looked as I'd seldom looked before, peering through the latticework with my 7x35 binocular. I kept the glass still, moving only my eyes until I'd scrutinized all the shades of gray and brown, all the shapes and shadows in the field. Then I would shift the Bausch & Lomb to another sector and start over. After glassing all around, I'd move slightly, and the details would have to be identified again. Changing place, even a little, changes your perspective and opens a new jungle to your eye.

After a very long time and not much progress, I shot the buck just in front of his ear, through an alley not much bigger than the diameter of a fly reel. He dropped so fast, the blur of recoil was all I saw, the clap of the .308 all I heard. It was the end of a pure hunt, one of few I've pulled-off successfully.

A lot of hunters shoot deer these days. Not many hunt them. Gary Lewis hunts deer, and his enthusiasm for the sport comes through in these pages. In plain, unembellished prose, he tells you what he likes about deer hunting as he tells you how to become a better deer hunter. I like the humility of this writer, his appreciation for the outdoors, and his perspective on hunting. Anyone who describes deer as "beautiful and graceful wild creatures" has my attention. As editor of *Mule Deer Magazine,* I've become weary of "185 bucks." Deer weren't born digital. They don't have anything to do with the scoring systems we've imposed on their antlers. They don't have any idea why men shoot at them, or that big antlers have been given a value above that of the hunt.

Gary Lewis might agree with me that for many hunters the ownership of a trophy—be it big antlers or an award for big antlers—has become more important than the chase. I suspect he thinks differently about the hunt. You can see it in his accounts of trails taken and deer shot. If you want to read only about outsize bucks taken on limited permits or in places open only to the privileged, you'll be disappointed here. But if instead you're looking for solid, plain-spoken information on wild deer and fair-chase hunting, if you want practical tips on finding the best spots and understanding deer movements, you're in the right place. There's advice on camping, shooting, and taking care of venison. No matter where you hunt in the West, this book has something for you. Gary takes you with him to Alaska for Sitka blacktails and hands you over to the capable Ed Park for Coues deer in the Desert Southwest. In between, where mule deer vanish on sage flats and slip unseen through alpine passes, you'll find the kind of reading worth reading again.

Because Gary Lewis is a hunter.

Books by Wayne Van Zwoll

Mastering Mule Deer, North American Hunting Club, 1988, hardback, 282 pp. $24.95

America's Great Gunmakers, Stoeger Publishing, 1992, softcover, large format, 280 pp. $16.95

Elk Rifles, Cartridges and Hunting Tactics, self-published, 1992, hardback, 416 pp. $24.95

Modern Sporting Rifle Cartridges, Stoeger Publishing, 1998, softcover, large format, 310 pp. $21.95

The Hunter's Guide to Ballistics, The Lyons Press, 2001, softcover, large format, 280 pp. $29.95

Elk and Elk Hunting, Safari Press, 2001, hardback, large format, 384 pp. $44.95

The Hunter's Guide to Accurate Shooting, The Lyon's Press, 2002, hardback, 340 pp. $29.95

The Gun Digest Book of Sporting Optics, Krause Pub., 2002, softcover, large format, 304 pp. $24.95

All books are available from the author at 2610 Highland Drive, Bridgeport, WA 98813. Autographed on request. Include an additional $3 per book for shipping.

Mule deer buck. Photo by Eric Hansen.

Chapter 1

DEER AND PRONGHORN ANTELOPE

MULE DEER

Beyond the end of the road there is a canyon. Vine maple, cottonwoods and willows grow along the stream. Junipers grow on the
shoulders of the ridge. The rimrock hides a trickle of water that
seeps out of a crack in the rock. Lichens encrust the surface of the stone
and there is a coolness that the rock holds even in the warmest months.

There are tracks at the little spring. Bighorn sheep and chukar water here.
Mule deer come to this water too. At least the old bucks do. Does, fawns, and
forkhorns take their water and feed from the valley.

The big bucks make their beds up tight against the rock walls of this
canyon, the next, and others like it for miles. Some of these bucks will live
out their lives in these canyon strongholds, only glimpsed at a distance by
some shepherd or cowboy looking for his stock.

Sometimes the stockman tells a hunter about the wide-racked buck he
saw. Mostly he doesn't.

The mule deer is the classic big game animal symbol of the west. It can
be found everywhere from the forested Cascades in Washington and Oregon,
east to the Great Plains, from Canada to Baja, California in Mexico. Its name
is taken from its large ears, which resemble those of a mule.

It is the largest of the three main species of North American deer. Overall body size varies with the region, available food, water, and genetics. Mature bucks can weigh up to 300 pounds or more.

Its coat is typically blond or red-gold in summer and gray in winter, and has a white patch below the throat. Mule deer have an identifying black patch which comes down the face from between the ears to a point below the eyes. Its hooves are larger and more blunt than other deer, allowing them to negotiate snow and rugged ground.

The mule deer's tail is smaller than the blacktail or whitetail's flag. It is white and thin in comparison, with a black tassel at the end. In build, the muley is muscular and blocky, though graceful.

Mule deer antlers are highly prized among North American hunters. Spread and mass are bigger than that of a whitetail or a blacktail. Typically, main beams fork into two branches, each branch forming two tines. Westerners call this buck a four-point. Eyeguards, if present, are shorter than the average whitetail's.

Although mule deer can be seen living in and around many western cities, the mature adult buck is difficult to hunt. He is an animal of the high country or open plains. Secretive, he makes his living in a rugged land, subsisting on twiggy flora, broad-leafed plants, and grasses. Only in the breeding season does he lose a bit of that natural wariness, sometimes traveling tens of miles in search of willing does. In much of the mountain west, the rut begins in early November. Farther south, it may fall in December or January.

Mule deer bucks grow antlers in their second year. Often a set of spikes, a spike, and a fork or forks. In his third year, the buck might grow a wispy three- or four-point rack. Much of the western buck harvest consists of these younger deer.

In his fourth year, the mule deer begins to grow the size of antlers for which he is famous. During the next few years of his life, antler spread will go from 20 inches upwards to 30 inches and beyond. A very few bucks will grow antlers in excess of 40 inches wide. At the end of his years, antler growth begins to diminish. What was once a magnificent buck with up to six points or more per side may become a two-point again, albeit with a great spread and noble appearance.

Mule deer shed their antlers in February or March. Shed antlers can be found in deer wintering habitat at low elevations. Migratory muleys spend summer and fall in the higher elevations escaping heat, flies, and predators. When snow flies at the onset of winter, they move to winter range.

BLACKTAIL DEER

The road was closed a few years ago by a gate. A timber company owns the lock. In the fall, a hunter might park his rig at the bottom and go in on foot. There is a patchwork of clear cuts and 30-year-old timber. Alder grows along the creek, and oak trees grow on the south-facing slope.

Gray squirrels skitter in the fallen leaves. Mountain quail and ruffed grouse take their gravel from the old logging road. Blackberry vines are growing over the skid roads as nature reclaims the land. There are bear tracks in the mud with water seeping into them.

Blacktail does and fawns feed on apple trees at the edge of town. Wise old bucks with nut-brown antlers may come in too, but only after dark. They return well before dawn to their safe pockets of cover.

Columbian blacktails are the deer of the Pacific Coast. Hunters find their tracks from California into Canada. A variant, called the Sitka black-tail can be found from British Columbia north and west to Kodiak Island in Alaska.

In body size Sitka deer are on average smaller than their mule deer cousins, though some specimens of outsize Columbians and Sitkas are taken. Most blacktails won't exceed 200 pounds in body weight. Sitka bucks average 100 to 150 pounds, For more information on hunting Sitka deer, see Chapter 8.

In coloration, blacktails go from red-gold in summer to gray and brown in their winter coats. Ears are smaller than mule deer ears. Like the mule deer, a blackish patch can be found between the eyes. Antler conformity is similar to the mule deer, but smaller. Antler spread typically ranges from 15 to 23 inches.

The blacktail's flag is similar in shape to that of a whitetail deer, but not as long. It is brown at the base and predominantly black, shaped like a willow leaf. The underside is white. The blacktail

A big blacktail buck is considered to be one of the most difficult trophies in North America. Photo by Eric Hansen.

has a white throat patch. Many Sitka deer have a double throat patch.

Among Sitka deer, a three-point buck is the norm for a mature adult deer. Antlers are smaller than Columbian blacktails. Any four-point Sitka is considered a real trophy.

Blacktails eat twiggy browse, succulent forbs, grasses, and nuts. With snow on the ground, you may find their tracks on a lonely saltwater beach where they have been feeding on kelp.

Young forests are the best places to find large numbers of blacktails. One to ten years after a fire or a logging operation has passed through, blacktails will thrive. A mix of various ages of timber and types of foliage provide the food and shelter the deer require throughout the year.

The blacktail rut begins in the first week of November and continues into December. The best bucks are normally taken during the rut, when their good judgement is cast to the wind. In November, blacktails are vulnerable to rattling and calling.

Fawns are born in the spring. A sunny spring provides the photosynthesis that enriches the plant life with the nutrients that will see the young deer through the coming winter. Predators take their toll on the young.

Bucks shed their antlers in late winter. The sheds can be found on forest trails and at fence crossings. These clues provide a better understanding of the quality of local deer than the sheds found on mule deer winter range. Blacktails aren't as migratory as mule deer because most blacktails live in more temperate climates.

Due to his secretive ways, a mature blacktail buck, whether his antlers make 'book' or not, is a prize that any hunter can be proud of. And a truly big blacktail may be one of the toughest trophies of all.

WHITETAIL DEER

The river falls gently there, a series of light rapids flow through farmland. There is a cornfield irrigated with river water. The fertile land grows wheat on the benches overlooking the valley. A narrow strip of cottonwoods and oak trees line the river.

The tracks of valley quail can be found at the edge of the cornfield. Hungarian partridge and pheasants are relative newcomers to these parts, and so is the whitetail deer that calls this bottomland home.

Does and fawns, comfortable in close proximity to man, feed in the fields at harvest time, move out of the way of the tractor, and prowl around the silos at night. The bucks are secretive, and careful. Intimate with their home turf, they have multiple escape routes when danger approaches.

The whitetail has claimed the bottomland in much of the west, pushing mule deer into the hills. They are the smallest of the three major deer species and are divided into many subspecies according to locale. The Coues deer, pronounced 'cows' or 'coos'—depending on who you talk to—is found in Mexico, New Mexico, and Arizona. This subspecies averages little more than 40 pounds. Ed Park has hunted Coues deer for many years. See Chapter 9 for his techniques for hunting the "Gray Ghost of the Southwest".

An animal comfortable living in close proximity to man, concealment is the whitetail's best defense. Photo by Ed Park.

Oregon protects a whitetail subspecies called the Columbian whitetail. It was recognized as endangered in 1967. Efforts are underway to restore populations in the Umpqua Basin and on some Columbia River islands.

The antlers of the whitetail consist of a single main beam on each side with projecting tines. Eyeguards, or brow tines, are longer than the muley's. The most distinguishing characteristic of the whitetail is its tail. Full and brown on the outside, its underside is white. The upraised flag of its tail in escape is becoming a more common sight in much of the west.

The whitetail is an animal of timbered, brushy, or swampy country. Not prone to migration, it will spend most of its life within a few square miles of the same area. Nocturnal, it feeds mainly at night. Early morning and late evening are the best times to find a buck.

Concealment is the whitetail's best defense. In the presence of danger, the buck will either hold tight or sneak away from its pursuer.

The western hunter seeking to complete his hunting education, should not ignore the whitetail. This graceful, cautious deer makes a fine trophy and good table fare.

AXIS DEER

The tall grass blows in the wind that comes off the ocean. Kiawe trees grow where the beach sand ends. A spotted deer with tall three-point antlers is bedded in the shade, waiting for the sun to set.

Antlers, ears, nose, and eyes are visible in and around the trees: deer, bedded in the shadows beneath the overhanging branches. They find their feed on open plains, tall grass, and succulent forbs that grow in the sunny climate of the island.

Some years there is more water, some years there is less. The deer find it in streams that run when the rain falls and in deep pools that hold water when little can be found elsewhere.

There are more deer than most of the island's visitors and residents know about. They can be found in the lowland scrub near the ocean, in desert-like terrain on the western side, and in rain forest in the uplands.

Sometimes their tracks can be found along the roads or beaches, but most deer find refuge away from habitation where they are seldom seen by human eyes.

Axis deer are animals that prefer the safety of the herd, are nocturnal, and communicate by vocalization.

Axis deer were introduced to the Hawaiian Islands in 1868. Native to India, a small herd of the animals were a gift to King Kamehameha V from the Hawaiian Consul in Hong Kong. Initially they were established on the island of Molokai. Subsequent herds have been founded on Lanai and Maui.

Axis bucks stand three and a half feet at the shoulder and average 150 to 160 pounds as adults. Females average 90 to 100 pounds on the hoof.

Their coats are golden brown, flecked with white spots from neck to tail. On throat and belly, the hair is cream-colored, and a black dorsal stripe runs along the spine.

Bucks grow unique, three-pronged antlers that can reach lengths of 30 inches in the main beam and over 20 inches wide. A hunter can always find these animals in various stages of antler growth. Axis deer breed throughout the year.

Hawaiian axis deer can be hunted on public grounds in March and April and on private land throughout the year. Axis deer can also be hunted on some

Axis deer can be hunted on several Hawaiian Islands and on private ranchlands in Texas. Photo by garykramer.com

ranches in Texas. The elusive quality of the animal, combined with its singular beauty and good-tasting meat, makes the spotted deer from India a worthy trophy. See Chapter 10 for specific information on hunting axis deer.

PRONGHORN ANTELOPE

The dirt road ends at a broken-down rock fence built long ago by a rancher. From there the hunter must go afoot on this high mesa. Silver-green sage-brush flats extend as far as the eye can see. Horses still run wild, and sage grouse share the water holes.

On the slope of a rolling rise, a small band of pronghorn antelope have bedded. The ground breaks off sharply behind them and their view of the valley is commanding.

The small herd stands to its feet as the buck wheels around the perimeter, appearing orange and white against the sage. Now, with his herd trotting over the hill and down into the canyon, he pauses to look back, his horns shiny and black in the morning sun.

The pronghorn antelope is a species unique to the continent of North America. It is found in greatest numbers in the United States with Wyoming being home to approximately one-third of the antelope population.

As one of the smallest big-game species, does average 65 to 70 pounds and bucks average 100 pounds. Both males and females may have horns, though does' horns may not develop until later in life.

Pronghorn horns are unique in the animal kingdom. A bony, fibrous core is concealed by a pronged, outer sheath which is shed in the fall. The horns of the doe usually do not exceed the length of the ear. Males and females can be distinguished by the female's absence of the dark blaze on the cheek. Only bucks have this prominent black cheek patch. Does are light colored along the bridge of the nose with black occurring at the tip. The face of a buck appears black from forehead to tip of nose.

White bellies and rump patches help this creature stand out from other animals. They are tan across the back, hips, and shoulders. From the front, they appear striped with alternating tan and white on neck and brisket.

The rump patch is used as a signal to other antelope. When danger is identified, the animals flash their rump hairs erect to warn the others in the band.

Pronghorn tracks can be differentiated from deer tracks on moist ground. Prints are wedge-shaped and there is no dewclaw as found on deer or elk.

Vision and speed are the pronghorn's best defense. Antelope key on movement at long distances. Their phenomenal vision contributes to many blown stalks during hunting seasons. When they decide to run, they can move at speeds in excess of 60 miles per hour and sustain that speed until the dust trails track them far out of sight.

Pronghorn buck.
Photo by Eric Hansen.

Pronghorns eat low shrubs and weeds and will feed on some cactus. They prefer rolling plateaus and plains cut by gullies. They are found at higher elevations in the summer and in the valleys when snow is on the hills.

A herd will stick to a defined range within a radius of about ten to fifteen miles. Their greatest enemy is the coyote, which does the most damage in the spring when fawns are young.

The breeding season, or rut, runs from the end of August through September, coinciding with hunting seasons in many states.

The pronghorn is a public-land trophy that all hunters can pursue without great expense. The pursuit will leave you with an experience like hunting no other game animal, making you a better hunter and leaving you with unforgettable memories. Handled properly, his meat is fantastic.

To learn more about hunting pronghorns, turn to Chapter 11.

Gary Lewis with an opening day 4-point he took on the edge of a treeless plain.

Chapter 2

LOCATION, LOCATION, LOCATION!

Evaluating Country

ONE OF MY GOOD HUNTING partners is James Flaherty. His uncle owned ten acres at the base of a huge canyon that was blacktail heaven during hunting season. The only way in was through James' uncle's place. One season James was starting a new business and had plans to bowhunt for elk while I made the arrangements for opening weekend.

What I didn't know was how much time James would spend elk hunting during archery season, or how many hours he would be putting in at the office away from his family. These things were immaterial to me at the time. I was going deer hunting, . . . or so I thought.

Three days before the season, Denise Flaherty, James' wife, told him in no uncertain terms that he better plan on being home for the weekend. There would be no negotiation.

When I got the call, I said the things that a friend says when his wife explains how things are going to be. But when I hung up I went into panic mode.

I had to bounce back quick. This was Wednesday and the season was starting on Saturday. I had to have a map!

Southwest Oregon was my first choice. I was looking for public access and a place where there were no roads. I looked at several maps before I found what I wanted.

There were two mountains with a saddle between them. Roads ran parallel to the saddle but almost a mile separated them.

It was a roadless area with high ground for bedding, feeding, and escape trails. I drew an "X" between the mountains in the middle of that saddle. I laid my map on the counter, knowing I had found my deer. 🦌

Just like in retail, restaurants, and real estate, when you go deer hunting, location is everything. Blacktail deer can be found throughout Western Washington, Oregon, and Northern California, but certain types of habitat will hold them in greater numbers. If you want to see blacktail deer, watch clearcuts. Logging operations benefit these animals because they open up the forest canopy to let in the sunshine. New growth springs up and deer can find most of what constitutes good habitat all in one place.

Remember, deer need food, water, shelter, and space. Sometimes they get all four in a clearcut. They also

Classic mule deer habitat—sagebrush and junipers. This mule deer doe was bedded high on the hill, watching the approach from below. Gary Lewis photo.

become vulnerable to hunters, which is why you'll find only does, fawns, and immature bucks in a clearcut.

If you want to fill your tag with an antlerless deer (when legal), or a young buck, hunt the clearcuts in the morning, bedding areas at noon, and paths leading from bedding areas in late afternoon. You will find the deer.

However, clearcuts are not as easy to find as they once were. Forest practices have changed. Now, chemicals are often used to control the growth of weeds—what we hunters refer to as forbs and what deer call groceries. Today's super-fast growing seedlings turn clearcuts into forests again a lot faster than they used to.

Also, fear of fire may keep gates closed to timber company lands in low-water years, with "No Access" signs posted until the rains come.

So the face of blacktail hunting is changing. Look at what the orange-clad horde is doing and do the opposite. Many hunters know only the old way of hunting: Drive gravel roads and watch the openings. Park in the landing of an old logging operation and watch the hillside. Or, hope that a buck dashes across the road on his way to the next clearcut. That's not the way to get satisfaction from the hunt. That's not the way to teach your son or daughter the ways of the forest.

Look for the pockets that the crowds pass by. Sometimes they may be so obvious no one would think to hunt there. Sometimes they are so far back in the woods not many will make the effort to get there. Sometimes the brush is so thick that other hunters detour so they won't get caught in it.

In these hideouts, big blacktail bucks grow old without ever being seen by a hunter during the season. Their sanctuaries provide both cover and food. Water can be obtained after dark.

The pocket might be 200 acres in size or half an acre (like the spot marked with the "X" on my map).

IT WAS THE SECOND DAY of the season and I was in cover so thick that it was impossible to see more than ten yards in any direction except straight up. Above me was blue sky. In fact, weeks without rain had so dried the forest, I couldn't take a step without it sounding like I was walking through a giant bowl of corn flakes.

There were deer feeding to my left. Seeking openings in the wall of brush, I tried to get a glimpse to see what they were. My tag allowed

Mule deer feeding in forest habitat. Gary Lewis photo.

me to take any buck with one forked horn or better. I was hoping for something better.

"Huck, huck, huck," a doe called to the other deer. I saw her for an instant, head down as she trotted toward the others.

Then I saw her again, and she saw me through the brush. There was only a distance of about eight yards between us. Not feeling threatened, she relaxed, flopped her ears, and looked over her shoulder at—I presumed—the other deer. Then she resumed feeding and began to come closer.

The wind was at the back of my neck as I faced her. Any moment she would smell me.

Suddenly, she caught my scent and swapped ends, bolted for safety, and alerted the other deer—still unseen in the brush. They crashed away and I was alone again.

I followed a deer trail, so well-used that the dirt looked and smelled like freshly-plowed soil. Uphill, I came to a rocky promontory. The deer I'd just spooked had gone around it to the left. I would cut to the right. If I could get up on top, there would be a view down into the brush ahead.

I started up, grabbed a handhold, found a spot for my toe, and pulled myself up hand-over-hand. Halfway up the cliff I was able to abandon rock climbing and step from boulder to boulder. The view was good. From up there I could see not only more brush, but the tops of the brush. A marked improvement. I looked out over an area that had burned years ago. Thick willows had grown up.

I rested against the rock wall. Something moved out there. A rattling of dry leaves. Closer to me a squirrel scampered, rustling among the dry twigs and fir cones.

The noise came again. Too big for a squirrel. A bear? I held my breath as the willows moved. Three tall firs obstructed my field of vision. There. Antlers! Wide antlers with heavy beams.

I raised my rifle and waited for him to show. I felt the wind in my face. Good, he shouldn't smell me. I eased along the rocky ledge, trying for a clearer view of the deer just 70 yards away.

Suddenly he lifted his head and looked directly at me through the branches of a fir tree. If I waited a moment more, he'd be gone, crashing away through the willows.

I snicked the safety off, steadied the crosshairs, and touched the trigger, feeling the rifle recoil. The echo of the shot rang from the hills and my empty brass tinkled down through the rocks as I loaded another cartridge— just in case.

I found him where he fell. A four-point blacktail. He'd lived well in this thick cover which doubled as food.

I marked my tag and tied it around the antler beam. My season, and my quest for a big blacktail, was finished. And now, a long way from the road, the hard work would begin. As I cleaned the deer, I heard voices. Two hunters were talking about their morning. Their voices came to me on the breeze.

As I listened, the conversation grew fainter as the hunters changed direction to avoid the brush that gave up a buck so big that it would have made their eyes pop. 🌿

While young blacktails take their chances in the clearcuts and big black-tails go nocturnal, mule deer often use space and obstacles to escape hunters. Muleys use an escape mechanism called stotting to evade preda-tors. The stott is that familiar, stiff-legged bounce that western hunters know. The muley uses it to put stuff between him and the pursuer. Bounding over and around stumps, boulders, fallen trees and fences, the muley knows it is the most effective means of quick escape.

Big mule deer also seem to know that sometimes movement gives them away. (My good friend and hunting partner, Ryan Eicher, tells of the time he watched a trophy muley belly-crawl over the top of a butte while another hunter stood there oblivious, only fifty yards away. Ryan watched, helpless, from the top of another butte.)

Mule deer and mule deer hunters are fond of drier climates. Muleys make their living in open sage country, juniper and pine forests, farmland and towns. Watch for them along the river bottoms or in the high rimrocks.

Location is key. Mule deer country is big. Deer may be anywhere, but some places are far better than others.

Where do the deer feed? Since bottom land provides good fare for deer, you will often find large herds in the fields at first light. There are almost always a few small bucks hanging around a large herd. Access may be hard to obtain in most mule deer country these days, but you can always find a herd that feeds on private land and beds on public ground. Set up between feeding and bedding areas and you may be able to fill your tag.

You are not going to find bragging-size bucks in these situations before the rut. To take a woods-wise muley buck, you need to look up the canyons. All he needs to survive is there. Bitterbrush, wild plum, sage, and a few broadleaf plants and grasses make up the bulk of his diet. If there is water close by and a couple of escape routes, he has it made—until you come along.

Now you are looking for places far from any road. Again, sniff out those pockets where big deer can hide throughout the season from most hunters. Most hunters won't go more than a half-mile from the road where they parked the truck. Many won't travel more than 300 yards from their transportation.

And most hunters want to be out of the woods before dark. Most hunters will never see a big buck. They simply limit their chances of success because they haven't taken the time to learn to use map and compass and are afraid to get lost. Don't be like most hunters.

Study the map to determine likely feeding-to-bedding travel routes. Try to pick out possible escape routes.

Where would your buck bed? Probably up against a rock wall or under a tree where there would be some shade in the afternoon. It would be a place where he could see other deer, a place where he could observe predators. A high place with at least two escape routes. No wild animal wants to be trapped.

Water would be close by. Typically, a mule deer won't travel more than

800 yards from his source of water. Where are the springs and seeps? Are there natural catch basins that might hold water? What about streams? A deer needs water and mule deer country can make a creature thirsty.

It's important to know how to find mule deer country on a map. So is a good conversation with the local wildlife biologist. Those people know where the deer are. They also know why they're there. I've learned more from talking to a biologist for a half an hour than I used to learn in a whole season on my own.

The key is asking the right questions. They are public servants. They are there to serve the public well for the good of the wildlife. In most cases they're hunters themselves. Treat them

Two technicians watch a controlled burn. Natural and controlled burns foster new growth. Pay attention to such places when you find them. The deer and elk will. Gary Lewis photo.

with the respect their education and experience deserves.

Ask about previous winters' winter-kill. Ask about fawn production. Ask about buck–to–doe ratios. Are they reaching their management objectives? Ask which corners of the units they manage are the most productive. After asking, shut up and let them talk. There is no need to impress them with your experience or how much you know. Be friendly and thank them for their time. These men and women can be your most valuable resource.

Mule deer are also found in timbered country. I have hunted a good deal in a sub-alpine setting. The land is broken. Run-off streams have cut channels and canyons. The country is characterized by meadows, pumice fields, and lava rock. Long timbered ridges provide travel corridors and bedding cover.

What I like best about these areas are their good edge-habitat. The deer bed in the tall pines, among the younger firs, in the twisted hemlocks up high, and out in the open on boulder-strewn slides. They bed in the manzanita on the lower slopes. Their passage can be *heard* in the dry leaves, but the head-high brush hides them well.

Its wilderness designation makes it harder to access than a lot of public hunting grounds. The end of August, early in archery season, you will find the bucks in the high country, still protective of their velvet-covered antlers. When scouting mule deer country, learn to look for nipped shrubs. Take the time to observe feeding deer and get a look at what they're browsing on.

Shed antlers can give clues to the size and number of bucks using the wintering grounds. Gary Lewis photo.

Mule deer feed primarily on browse, the young twiggy ends of small bushes, and trees. Forbs (broad-leafed flowering plants) their next favorite. Grasses, nuts, seeds, and moss round out their diet.

Mule deer can survive on little water. They prefer to take their water from springs, seeps, basins, ponds, and lakes. At the water's edge, they drink, take a look around, drink again and retreat into the trees. The noise of running water can mask the sounds of approaching predators. Find all the water sources.

MY FAMILY USED TO OWN PROPERTY in rural Southwest Washington. We owned a lake and had a long strip of frontage along the Lewis River. When I could get away from cutting brush, I used to track the deer. I'd find a few tracks of small deer, does, and fawns at the river's edge. Way down in the swamp I found a spring and a little pool. The sandy soil at its edge was littered with tracks. The bigger deer weren't taking chances at being caught out in the open. They took their water deep in the woods where no one could see them. 🦌

Deer keep moving while they feed. It keeps their noses in the wind and lessens the likelihood of being taken by a predator. When deer travel together, one animal—usually a doe—takes the lead and watches for danger while the other deer feed. Note the direction that the animals are feeding. In the evening, they're usually feeding away from their beds. Mornings, they'll feed toward their beds.

A muley may not bed in the same place each day, but you will find that most big bucks have just a few choice hideaways.

Whitetail hunters can make good use of these deer prospecting methods. Whitetails, maybe more so than blacktails and muleys, are animals that hold in pocket-type cover. Maps and aerial photos can help you select potential pockets in advance of the hunt.

It might be a small valley or a river bottom. Woodlands or swamplands adjacent to agricultural fields are good bets. Walk the country well before the season opener and look for deer run-

The deer were spotted mid-morning on the far slope of this western Oregon clearcut. After a long stalk, a successful shot was made, followed by a long pack trip out. Closed roads kept vehicle-bound hunters out. Gary Lewis photo.

ways and evidence of browsing. Look for the main trails then try to pinpoint the secondary, parallel trails that big bucks use. Find a way to physically look into your pocket from nearby vantage points.

Look for all the elements that a deer needs to survive—the food, water, shelter and space that create an ideal habitat for a deer herd. In and around these holding areas, you can find the pockets where the bigger bucks live.

Larry Monger with a 3-point blacktail he took in Southwest Oregon's archery season. The blacktail's antlers measured over 19 inches wide.
Photo courtesy Larry Monger.

Chapter 3

THE CHASE
AND THE
SPIRIT OF THE HUNT

FAIR CHASE

The concept of giving the game "a sporting chance" is almost as old as hunting itself. It springs from the ethic of a skilled hunter who appreciates the challenge of the hunt almost as much as the meat or the trophy.

When the elusive, wild, big game animal is hunted within the law and subdued through a hunter's skill, the meat and the trophy has more meaning for the hunter.

Theodore Roosevelt, a founder of the Boone and Crockett Club, brought the concept of Fair Chase to the attention of the sporting public in the early 1890s. The rules of Fair Chase, as set forth by Boone and Crockett, have been expanded to exclude technological aids. Fair chase, as defined by the B&C Club, is the ethical, sportsmanlike and lawful pursuit and taking of any free-ranging wild, native North American big game animal in a manner that does not give the hunter an improper advantage over such game animals.

The best known record-keeping organizations are the Boone and Crockett club (firearms and archery) and the Pope and Young club (archery). Records of trophy animals are kept, but the real value of these clubs is the promotion of the Fair Chase ethic.

Neither club will recognize trophies that were taken after spotting or herding from the air, followed by landing in the vicinity for the purpose of pursuit and shooting. Herding or chasing game with a motor vehicle is also prohibited.

More hunters now use radios to stay in communication with their party. The use of radios as an aid in the taking of game is outside the bounds of Fair Chase. Artificial lighting, night vision, and heat-sensing devices will exclude trophies taken with such aids from recognition in the record book.

The trophy was not taken under the rules of Fair Chase if it was enclosed within an artificial barrier such as an escape-proof fence or transplanted for the purpose of commercial shooting. Nor will the animal qualify for recognition if killed while swimming or helpless in deep snow.

It is also outside the rules of Fair Chase if the trophy was harvested on another hunter's license or not in full compliance with the game laws or regulations of the federal government, state, province, territory, or tribal council.

Think about the trophy that you would like to bring home. Your standards might not be as high as Boone and Crockett's, but it is your trophy just the same. How will you feel if you look at an antlered head and

Gary Lewis perched on the back of a friend's 4-wheeler. The 4-wheeler is a tool that is useful for transportation and packing meat. Use it thoughtfully, with regard for others and the habitat. Gary Lewis photo.

recall that the animal wasn't taken fairly?

Earn the skill of a hunter, then pursue your quarry. Sure, you could *buy* a trophy, but money is a poor substitute for skill.

Turn to the back of any outdoor magazine and read the classified ads. Sprinkled among the antelope, blacktail, Coues deer, mule deer, and rocky mountain elk hunts, you will see ads for whitetail, exotics, and elk that boast of the outfitter's "No-Kill, No-Pay" guarantee. This is the first clue that you might be looking at a "put-and-take" operation-run behind a high fence for animals transplanted or artificially enhanced for their "trophy" quality. You need to know before you go.

These hunting operations have their place in a free society. Some are quality outfits built on ethics and a good reputation. Some are not. They are hunts that take place within a controlled environment. More than likely, you will bag your animal. Success rates are high because the outfitter does not get paid unless you take home a trophy.

A preserve hunt is usually quicker than a "fair chase" hunt. Safety is one factor people cite in their decision to hunt on a preserve. Hunter numbers are limited so there is less chance an accident could occur. In the event of a medical emergency, help is not far away. Preserve hunts can also be adapted to suit the needs of handicapped hunters.

In the quest for a trophy blacktail, mule deer, or whitetail, either a guided or self-guided hunt can be an adventure of a lifetime. Many are the potential memories that await you in the classified sections of the hunting magazines or the booths at sportsman's shows. Decide what you want from your hunt before you book a trip. Just don't let your desire for a trophy cloud good judgment.

ETHICS AND MANNERS

The best examples of bad manners among sportsmen can now be found among the crowd that uses Four-wheelers. Four-wheelers are loud, brash, and rude. So are some of the people who use them. Now don't get me wrong. I've ridden a four-wheeler up an old road in hunting season, parked at the trailhead, hiked in, and liked it.

Four-wheelers have saved me sleep, wear and tear on my knees, and hours of hunting time. I've been to places that I never would have seen otherwise. Yes, they have a place in big-game hunting, but some hunters take it too far.

ONE SEASON, I HUNTED in one of eastern Oregon's finest elk hunting units. Most often, we hunted the wilderness area, parked on the edge and hiked in. On the third day, we went exploring new country. The road ended in a little clearing that passed for a parking lot and trailhead. We parked and headed out along a trail that would bring us to a canyon where we were planning to make our evening hunt.

Two miles from the trailhead, we began to feel that we were in elk country. We found tracks crossing the trail, beds on a rocky outcropping, and fresh sign. Then, on the wind came the sound of an engine. We heard it come closer and closer until finally two rifle-toting hunters drove into view on a Polaris. They were dressed in matching bib–overalls and hats. Each had piercing blue eyes, but the passenger had a lot more gray in his mustache.

"Seen any elk?" (The universal question during late October.)

"Nope."

They were headed for the same canyon we had in mind—and they would get there a lot quicker; but the sound of their engine would keep the animals in the timber until well after dark.

They traveled on. We turned around and headed back to the truck.

We had parked our four-wheeler at the trailhead. They had passed it on the way. With no concern that they might ruin someone else's hunt, they charged ahead.

Such are the encounters you sometimes have on public land. 🐾

Just because the machine will carry you there doesn't mean you should use it in every situation. If someone is hunting the area you intended to hunt in, don't go roaring by. Show some regard for others. Hunting is not a motorcross event. Park your ATV and go in under your own power.

Some of the best hunting memories can result from hunting camp. Pick the wrong partners, though, and you may have a trip that is hard to forget. A few words to the wise. Don't hunt with alcoholics—a little whiskey or wine after dinner doesn't hurt anyone, but heavy drinkers shouldn't be welcome. Too many things can go wrong out in the woods.

Besides having a few too many drinks, another way to ruin the experience is to bring along a lazy hunter who believes other people should do his work for him. Each hunter should take their turn at cooking, washing the dishes, and getting firewood.

WHEN I WAS FOURTEEN, my dad and I waded a river to hunt blacktail deer on a large island. It was my first season hunting big game and I was excited. I guessed, the island would be teeming with deer and we'd have them all to ourselves.

Dad waited at the river while I hunted along the edge of a stand of cottonwoods. I was moving quietly, turning my head this way and that, watching for a buck.

"Sssst."

I froze. The sound had come from above me. I looked up into the eyes of an old hunter. I had picked a good spot.

This mule deer buck was photographed at a State Park in Eastern Oregon. Practice field-judging techniques when you have the opportunity. The tips of a mule deer's ears are approximately 22 inches apart. An average mule deer has antlers measuring between 22 and 25 inches wide and 15 inches tall. Gary Lewis photo.

Unfortunately, it was someone else's good spot. I mouthed the word, "Sorry," and headed back the way I'd come. 🦌

If someone has taken the time to scout a tree stand location, and if they're in the tree stand when you get there, find someplace else to hunt. On the other hand, if you find a stand in a likely spot on public land and no one else is around, feel free to hunt the area. Just don't use or tamper with someone else's tree stand.

WHEN I FIRST BEGAN hunting in Oregon's western deer rifle season, I was amazed at the number of rifle shots I would hear. Sometimes I thought everyone must be seeing deer but me.

One day I heard three, quick shots close by. I was less than a hundred yards from the road where the shots had come from. I hiked over for a look. Standing there was a man holding a rifle. He waved as I came out of the woods.

"Did you get a deer?" I asked.

"Nope, but I got that can," he proclaimed proudly. 🦌

The time for target-shooting is before the season.

Most of the hunters I meet are ethical, upstanding, and conscientious. But a lapse in judgment can make the best hunter look like a slob.

The slob hunter is the biggest threat to good hunting. He is an easy caricature for the non-hunting public to visualize. The anti-hunters have seized this image and they use it against us.

Set the ground rules before opening day. No target shooting. No shooting over roads. No drinking until the guns are put away. No loud music in camp. No road-hunting. No display of dead animals on roof-tops or bumpers.

Another opportunity for hunters to present a good image to the public is en route to the hunt. Don't wear camouflage in the airport. Give some thought to your appearance when you travel. Wash the camo makeup from your face before you go to a restaurant.

The image we portray to landowners, law enforcement, children, neighbors, and our non-hunting friends will determine the future of our sport.

TROPHY ESTIMATION IN THE FIELD

The trophy quality of a legal deer is in the eye of the hunter. My first buck, a small forkhorn, was a trophy. The spikes that followed it were not. Today, the bleached skull and spindly little antlers of my first forkhorn still remind me of that late September morning.

For most people, their first deer was a trophy, whether or not it had antlers. Those of us who have had some success afield should remember what it was like to take that first deer.

What is a trophy then? The dictionary defines it as anything taken in hunting and preserved as a memento. Some of my deer trophies are just preserved in photos. Others are racks or shoulder mounts hanging on the wall. So, a trophy hunter is the person who takes the time and effort to preserve some memento of the hunt. If that makes me a trophy hunter, then so be it!

Every hunter has their own standards as to what constitutes a trophy animal—one worth shooting, gutting, skinning, and bringing home to butcher. A few years ago, any legal animal was good enough for me.

Today, I pass on smaller bucks and wait for a deer with antlers as wide or wider than its ears. I may not always fill my tag. If it is a blacktail, a mature three-point will make me happy. If I'm hunting mule deer, then I will wait for a four-point buck.

Toward the end of the season, any legal buck is apt to put a smile on my face and an itch in my trigger finger.

These are the standards I've set for myself. Someday I may change them again, but I will probably never set them very high. I value venison steaks too much for that, and 'Old Mossyhorns' isn't known for the tenderness of his meat.

WHEN I FIRST SAW THE BLACKTAIL buck that I took in 1999, his head was down, polishing his antlers on a small fir tree. As I watched, he lifted his nose and nibbled at the tender new growth on the brush that towered above his head. A nice buck. This was the one. I lifted the rifle, waited for a clear shot and took it.

My first priority was to take care of the meat, but as I field dressed the deer I remembered what I had heard other hunters say about taking a nice buck: the antlers seem to shrink once the animal is on the ground. I looked again at the head. No, they hadn't shrunk. This was a good one. In fact, I guessed he would make the Oregon Big Game Record Book.

It was a blacktail buck in the prime of his life. He was sleek and heavy in the body. It took two hours to drag him out to the road. His head sported a four-by-four rack plus eyeguards. The antlers were almost perfectly symmetrical. 🦌

Blacktail and mule deer antlers are similar in conformity. Mature animals of both species have front forks that branch from the main beam. They may have eye guards as well.

Boyd Iverson, in his fine book, *Blacktail Trophy Tactics II,* [*see page 206] wrote, "A very large, mature blacktail buck has antlers which measure 16 to 20 inches across and sports four points on each side. He will sometimes have eye guards, but the lack of eye guards, even on mature bucks, is very common. His antler shape is similar to the mule deer, only smaller, and usually cages inward at the top. Many

The trophy quality of a legal deer is in the eye of the hunter. This is a 1-1/2 year old mule deer, photographed in Eastern Oregon. Gary Lewis photo.

times a set of antlers which has an outside spread of 16 to 20 inches will have an inside, tip-to-tip spread of only six or eight inches."

But all this is hard to judge in the woods. The best way to tell a trophy-size buck from an average deer is by looking at antlers in relation to ears. A blacktail buck's ears measure from 16 to 18 inches from tip to tip. This allows the hunter to quickly judge the size of an animal's rack.

The tips of a muley buck's ears are approximately 22 inches apart when standing erect. An average mature mule deer buck has antlers measuring between 22 and 25 inches wide and 15 inches tall. If the antlers appear to overlap the ears by four inches on each side, then you are looking at a buck that may reach the magical 30-inch spread.

Mule deer antlers begin to approach record-book size when good mass is achieved, they are wider than the ears and symmetrical, and are as tall as they are wide.

The tips of a Sitka blacktail's ears range between 15 and 15-1/2 inches apart. An average adult blacktail has a rack that is 14 to 16 inches wide. Average bucks have a rack half again as wide as it is tall. If you see a buck with antlers as tall as they are wide, you are looking at an above-average deer. Most have two- or three-point racks. Any Sitka deer with four or more points per side (not counting eyeguards), is a trophy.

Non-typical racks are special to many deer hunters. Any unusual rack may be a trophy. Some common features on these uncommon bucks are multiple brow tines, drop points, palmation, "stickers," or a second main beam. Use the amount of mass to determine whether this is a buck you want to take.

The ear width of a whitetail is between 15 and 18 inches. Bragging-size bucks have antlers that are the width of the ears. Look for heavy beams and at least four long tines on each side.

With good optics, pronghorn antelope can be easy to judge in the field. Again, decide what constitutes a trophy for you. A 12-inch buck is a good representative of the species, but an animal with 14-inch or longer horns is considered a trophy by many hunters.

A pronghorn's ears are about six inches long. If the horn is two-and-a-half times the length of the ear, and the prong is almost as wide as the ear is long, then you're looking at a good buck with 15-inch horns and a five-inch prong. If the width at the base of the horn appears to be three inches (or half the length of the ear), you should be planning a stalk.

The best way to learn to judge trophy animals is to look at a lot of them. Zoos, game farms, and hunting preserves offer ample opportunity. Try estimating trophy quality on individual animals and practice judging from various angles.

One of the side benefits of field-judging animals is that it helps you get over the adrenaline-induced shakes that sometimes accompanies the sighting of a trophy buck.

Develop a friendship with a taxidermist who will let you study trophies hanging in his shop. Study Boone and Crockett score sheets for a better idea of what constitutes a high-scoring buck.

Know what constitutes a trophy in the area you will be hunting. Some areas are known for producing outsize specimens. Other locations might not have the genetics or the minerals in the soil to produce big antlers.

Talk to guides, outfitters, landowners, fish and wildlife personnel, and law enforcement officers who are familiar with the area you plan to hunt. They know what the land is capable of producing.

Every animal is an individual and it takes more than reading from a book to judge antlered-game quickly. However, after investing time and study, you can become an accomplished field-judge of big game. Some bucks you will have to pass up if they don't meet the standards you set prior to your hunt. Your experience will be reflected in the trophies you bring home.

The best-known record keeping organizations are the Boone and Crockett club (firearms) and the Pope and Young club (archery). In Oregon, *The Record Book for Oregon's Big Game Animals*, is another book that lists the highest scoring animals taken in the state.

This book classifies Oregon blacktail deer in three distinct categories. The Northwest Blacktail are those that are found in the northwestern corner of the state. The Columbian Blacktail are those deer that inhabit the Willamette Valley, points south, and to the coast. The Cascade Blacktail live in the stretch of the Cascades with the Pacific Crest Trail and the Klamath-Jackson County division as the boundary line.

Trophies taken in the state of Washington are recorded in *The Record Book for Washington's Big Game Animals*. Scoring for the record books is done by measuring the height and width of the antlers, the length of the main beams, and the tines. Circumference of the antler beams are also measured, and points are deducted for lack of symmetry.

Taken in Jackson County, my Oregon blacktail buck is classified as a Cascade Blacktail. Sitting on a log, resting from the work of carrying a nearly 200-pound animal out of the woods, I used the two-inch ruler on my compass to make a measuring tape from the edge of my map. Stretching the map between the tips of the antlers I found an inside spread of 21 inches and an outside spread of 22.

To make the Oregon record book with a blacktail deer, the head must measure above 90 inches for an animal harvested with archery tackle and above 110 in the northwest corner for the firearms division. The minimum score for a Columbia or Cascade buck taken with a rifle is 125.

When my buck was finally "green-scored" he netted 139-1/8 inches. After a year he was measured again, for a final score of 137-5/8 inches.

Is this more special in my memory than my first buck or the first deer I took with my

Taken on public land in Southern Oregon, this blacktail's rack measured over 22 inches wide.
Gary Lewis photo.

bow? Probably not. But the harvesting of a trophy blacktail buck has been a goal of mine since I was a small child.

IN TWO DAYS OF STILL-HUNTING through old-growth timber and thick underbrush, I was able to close within a few yards of a number of deer—some I could see, others I only heard before some sound or shift in the wind alerted them to my presence.

For me, the challenges come in closing in on a wary animal, watching it feed and check its backtrail, watching it test the wind for the scent of a predator, and seeing how it reacts to the presence of other deer. Then finally letting the deer pass right by me without it ever knowing I was there. I wait for a clear shot and take it if the animal is a fine representation of his species and will provide a good supply of meat for my family through the winter. That's the kind of trophy I wait for. 🦌

Ed Park on Trophy Hunting and Record Books

The oldest and best known record book is *Records of North American Big Game*, from the Boone & Crockett Club, [250 Station Drive, Missoula, Montana, 59801; phone 888-840-4869; website: www.boone-crockett.org.] Their first record book was published in 1932, and the current (11th Edition) was published in 1999.

One thing I really like is the photos, especially those at the end of each species listing, showing hunters with their trophies. These are not necessarily photos of the highest-ranking trophies. For example, for "Coues deer, typical antlers," they show a lady with her 1994 buck that scored 110-7/8 points by the Boone & Crockett Club scoring system. The minimum point total needed is 110 points.

Such photos do at least two things. They prove that any trophy good enough to make any position in the record book is a really fine trophy, and although an animal is at the bottom of the listings, it is a truly magnificent trophy that anyone would be proud to have taken. Secondly, such photos let the rest of us see just how big a set of antlers or horns it takes to make the minimum book score.

A different scoring system is used for entry into the *Safari Club International Record Book of Trophy Animals*, published by Safari Club International, 4800 W. Gates Pass Road, Tucson, Arizona, phone: 520-620-1220, website: www.safariclub.org.

For bowhunters, the Pope & Young Club publishes *Bowhunting Big Game Records of North America*, which lists trophies taken with bow and arrow. Contact them at P.O. Box 548, Chatfield, MN 55923; phone 507-867-4144; website: www.pope-young.org.

The newest book of these four is the *Longhunter Muzzleloading Big Game Records Book*, published by the Longhunter Society, P.O. Box 67, Friendship, IN 47021; phone: 812-667-5131; website: www.nmla.org.

Even if you don't hunt with bow and arrow or muzzleloader, studying those books will help any hunter learn more about hunting, such as where trophy animals are taken.

—ED PARK

ATTITUDE

If there is one attribute a hunter can develop that will help him or her become a better hunter, it is confidence. It's what enables you to leave an hour before daylight while other hunters are warming their hands and lingering around the breakfast fire. It's what keeps you in the field at lunchtime while everyone else has headed back to camp for a sandwich. It is what tells you to keep hunting as the sun is setting, even though it means that you'll be late for the card game. It is that magic feeling that sets you apart from the orange-clad crowd. Cultivate it.

You want to know that wherever deer live, in whatever habitat you hunt them, you can solve the mysteries of the hunt, meet the challenge, and find a buck—and when found make the decision whether to shoot or not.

Nothing builds confidence like success. But success often comes hard the first few years. You need to make your own success.

It starts with research. Pick one area in the state you hunt and analyze it. Start with a map. Study the regulations, talk to hunters, and call wildlife biologists at the Department of Fish and Game. Are there good numbers of deer in the area? Are numbers stable or increasing? If the answers to these questions are positive, then focus on the types of habitat that the deer prefer. Then go scouting.

Sometimes the scouting may be camouflaged as other activities. Fishing, camping, Christmas tree cutting, horseback rides, mountain biking, vacations with the in-laws (optional), or even sales calls, can be used as cover for scouting trips. Watch the deer, take pictures of them, make notes in a journal. By applying methodology to your research, you are already becoming a better hunter.

Operate from a spirit of abundance not scarcity. Realize that there are enough deer spread among the good hunters—and the lucky. There may always be the lucky hunters, but luck runs both ways. Be a confident hunter and you'll eat more venison than the "lucky."

Find out what the harvest percentages are for the unit where you will be hunting. In much of the West, 25% of the hunters bring home their deer. By spending more days afield, your chances of being in that happy 25% will rise every hour you spend afield. Think of it as a numbers game. Stack the odds in your favor.

Practice shooting your weapon of choice at and beyond your effective range. Set a regular practice schedule and stick to it. Archers should be shooting every other day starting in April to be ready for the season openings in August and September. Rifle hunters should shoot at least once a month in the four months preceding rifle season. If rifle ammunition is too expensive, shoot .22 rimfire ammo. The key is in the steady training of the eye, breathing, and trigger pull.

Exercise builds endurance and confidence. If you hunt the backcountry, as I recommend in this book, you will work harder for your deer than the average hunter. You will also be far more successful than the average hunter.

Assemble and carry the gear necessary for survival. Become adept at using a compass, building fires in wet weather, and building shelters. If you ever spend the night unexpectedly in the backcountry, you need to know that you have the skills to survive.

If you will be hiking in and spending one night or more "in the bush," then you need to be in shape for the main event. When I worked in an office in downtown Portland, I ran the stairs at lunchtime and lifted weights in the evening.

These days, I do a little resistance training and focus my exercise on biking and running. I use a bike in much of my hunting to get beyond the road closures. If I see a buck two canyons over, I want to know that I can make a stalk, take my shot, recover the animal, and pack it out by myself.

Research, scouting, optimism, practice, survival skills, and exercise will make you a better hunter and give you the confidence to hunt deer anywhere.

Ed Park with a nice buck he tagged on a warm October evening. Gary Lewis photo.

Some of the West's best hunting can be found on public land. Gary Lewis photo.

Chapter 4

PROSPECTING FOR MULE DEER, BLACKTAILS, AND WHITETAILS

A doe peered back at me, framed against the evening sky by two tall ponderosa pines. Dale had seen her too and stopped, his back against a tree, camouflaged, blending with the bark and the needles.

As we watched, the doe wheeled and trotted, stiff-legged, back into the trees, taking a fawn and another doe with her. We found their paths where pine needles had been raked away to get at something. Trails converged in an intersection of sorts where the earth had been moved around to a depth of nine inches, creating a crater of sorts. A mineral lick or a dust bath?

Deeper into the trees, we bumped four more deer and watched them run away through the timber. The mottled sunlight played on their flanks as they ran.

As the sun moved to the horizon we climbed a ridge. Shadows lengthened and a breeze blew out of the west, filling the tops of the trees with sound. We looked for tracks, for nibbled branches along the trail, for the hollowed depressions of empty beds—for deer.

Forest foliage grows toward the sun, vertical lines reaching toward the sky. To spot deer, you look for parts of the animal, for the horizontal line of a back or the crook of a leg or the flick of an ear.

Dale spotted her first and stopped me with a whisper. Here was another doe. Her spring coat glistened with the sunlight that streamed through an opening in the trees. Today we were hunters again, though armed only with binoculars. We were searching out deer country for what we might learn. 🌿

The process of becoming a better hunter is one that takes a lifetime of study. Whether you hunt with bow and arrow, rifle, or camera. The principles are the same. To make the best shots, you need to watch the animals—to know their habits and preferences.

An animal needs shelter, space, food, and water to survive. The consistently successful deer hunter must understand how and where deer find and use these elements.

Rough, broken country makes for good mule deer habitat. Typically, does and fawns will be found at lower elevations, closer to the best food and water. Middle of the day finds them bedded, hidden in cool seclusion, or in open areas. Watch the edges of meadows for deer in morning and evening.

On the other hand, bucks prefer higher, more open country, as their tender antlers develop through the summer. When the weather is warm, look for their beds on cool north-facing slopes. But in order to find the animals, you also need to locate their nearby food.

The Pious Report, completed in 1989, found that a mule deer's diet consisted of 55% browse (the new growth of trees, shrubs, and vines with woody stems), 22% forbs (broadleaf plants), 10% grasses, 7% nuts, and 6% other materials.

Browse is abundant in mule deer habitat, but broadleaf plants are mule deer favorites. Locate these plants, confirm the deer are eating them and spend time watching in the morning and evening.

Deer take their water from ponds, puddles, creeks, rivers, lakes, seeps, and succulent plants. In another study researchers found that they travel an average of 800 yards to get it. They approach, ever watchful for predators—because coyotes, cougar, and other carnivores need water too.

Guide, riding for Oregon's Backcountry Outfitters, surveys an open meadow for game on a high-country pack trip. Gary Lewis photo.

It has been my experience that most deer live ordinary, average lives, moving in predictable patterns. You can see these deer day in and day out, crossing roads, streams, and feeding in open fields.

However, bigger bucks will not be found with the herd. They may live solitary lives or spend their days with one smaller buck that helps them watch for danger. The smaller buck is often sacrificed if a hunter comes too close.

The more experienced buck uses the land differently than his lesser brethren. He often feeds in marginal land, where making a living is harder but keeps him safer. Every bedding area has a back door. When moving from bed to feed, the smaller deer goes first. The only time he may let his guard down is during the rut. And then not for long.

Wise, old bucks don't cross roads or streams on long, open stretches. Instead, you will find their trails at bends in the road, where the chance of being seen for any length of distance is lessened. Often, they will not cross until after dark.

Deer use landmarks to help them move from one place to the next.

Cliffs, boulders, rock piles, and other obstacles serve as markers to traveling deer. These landmarks can be used during early season to gain a visual advantage over the surrounding terrain. When other hunters have deer on the move, a hunter can sit tight and wait for deer to move by on their escape from hunting pressure.

I MUSED ABOUT THIS as we picked our way off the ridge in the gathering darkness.

Dale caught a glimpse of another deer standing 100 yards off, ears cupped in our direction, watching. She turned and looked over her shoulder at another animal, then back at us. For fifteen minutes, she didn't move.

(Spring and summer provide great opportunities for observing deer in their habitat. We don't need to go far to find them and there's always something to learn. Don't get too close. Use a spotting scope, binoculars and a telephoto lens to bridge the distance. Does are bringing up their fawns in spring and summer, and their chance to build strength and reserves to see them through the winter.)

Watching through my binoculars, I felt rusty. Even as dark descended and we walked away, the doe waited in the trees. She was going somewhere, but in no hurry. I marveled at a life lived by seasons—not the second-hand of a clock. Months of working in the land of people, pressures, and pavement had squashed down the hunter inside me. I had forgotten that here, amid the pines and the cedar, the bitterbrush and the manzanita, time is of little importance.

MY GOOD FRIEND Grant Braun discovered early on the importance of hunting pockets. Wherever he hunts, he watches for the small pockets of cover that hold deer. While other hunters head far into the mountains and deserts, he hunts suburban bucks. In the 2000 season, he hunted in Central Oregon.

Through the spring and summer he had scouted and felt confident there were deer and elk using his patch of timber.

He had found a rectangular area, bordered on all four sides by roads and private land. A patchwork of small meadows, standing pines and abundant browse provided food, cover, and shelter for big game. The nearby river provided water.

He moved quietly in the pre-dawn light, picking his steps to make the least sound on the parched ground. This would be his first time hunting there, but he felt at home in the pines, in tune with the heartbeat of nature and his place in its balance.

The bow felt good in his hands. After months of practice, he was ready to use it for its intended purpose. In the past few years he had harvested two animals with his weapon—a 70-pound compound. Soon, he hoped, he would draw it again.

There was light enough to shoot as he made his way to the meadow and worked along the tree line and back out to the road. There were deeply cut tracks crossing the dirt road—the hoof prints of three deer. Grant guessed they were bucks traveling together.

This 4-point mule deer buck pursued his doe into this open field on a mid-November morning. Your post-season scouting trips during late fall and winter can help you learn more about the deer in your hunting area.
Gary Lewis photo.

He wasn't the only one after them. Down the road came two more hunters. The deer had just crossed the road as they came upon them. *There were three bucks in there,* the others hunters said.

Grant circled wide and entered the timber in front of the bucks, working again toward the other hunters.

Dead trees and branches littered the ground. The manzanita and bitterbrush grew tall so he could see no more than 40 yards in any direction. He nocked an arrow.

The buck had his head down, browsing, quartering toward Grant. He lifted his head. His antlers were narrow and tall, still encased in summer's velvet, his coat sleek and red. Grant watched for his chance, gauging the distance. He estimated 35 yards.

The buck turned then, giving Grant the shot he wanted. He drew, picking his spot behind the front shoulder. The arrow flashed away, connecting the hunter to the hunted.

As Grant admired his buck, the other bowhunters (his accidental hunting companions) walked up and helped him drag the heavy animal to the road only 60 yards away.

Since he started bowhunting, Grant has taken two other deer—blacktails—in similar conditions. Like the fisherman who specializes in pocket-water, Grant has been successful when he focuses on specific pockets of deer cover.

Most hunters know that the best hunting is in 'edge' habitat, those places where open spaces give way to pines, where pines give way to sage or manzanita. The outskirts of civilization pro-

Gary Lewis studies a topo map the evening before the hunt, hoping to find last-minute clues. Gary Lewis photo.

vide such habitat. Often, the ground is privately held, waiting to be brought into development. Such places have been logged at some point, allowing shrubs to thrive as trees are removed. This second-growth browse makes outstanding deer habitat.

Your best opportunity to cash-in on these close-to-home bucks is when the deer are undisturbed and following their normal routine. The deer spend their days bedded in clumps of bitterbrush, sage, or manzanita—sometimes surprisingly close to human habitation.

The key to finding these animals lies in recognizing what constitutes deer habitat. Focus on the small areas and understand that these deer are adaptable. They may prefer wide-open spaces, but they are making the best of what they've been given. Hunters, whether they hunt with bow or rifle, would do well to learn the same thing.

The key to my hunting success has been to find the pockets where deer spend most of their lives. Sometimes you find these pockets by "accident" (but you make this kind of accident happen by learning what to look for) and other times you find these pockets by studying maps with another hunter who has hunted the area in the past.

THE TOPS OF THE COTTONWOODS rattled with the wind. I watched leaves skitter across a dirt road. There were quail along the creek and chukar on the slopes above.

I scanned the edges of the cultivated land, glassed the tops of canyons, and looked under lone junipers in oceans of sage. I was looking for the black and white faces, the wide ears, and the polished antlers of a mule deer buck. I saw his trails on the hillside and found tracks of does, fawns, and bucks along the creek.

I took time out to taste an apple from a tree in the yard of an abandoned ranch. I drifted a grasshopper pattern along a cutbank where the long grass grew at the water's edge. A trout grabbed it, threw the hook, and moments later rose to the fly again. Simple pleasures.

But I was here to carry a rifle along those hillside trails, to prowl the juniper thickets and rimrocks for mule deer.

I wondered what tomorrow would bring as I stirred sliced steak and potatoes in the frying pan. I would be hunting the northern slope of a long ridge where there was water and browse for mule deer. I would find pastured cattle there as well.

A sliver of moon hung in the starry sky. I went to sleep to the sounds of laughter in the next camp. A man was playing a guitar and singing a song about how they don't write songs like that anymore.

It was a cold, hurried breakfast that fueled my start up the hill. The morning sun pushed back the shadows. I told myself to slow down—to be patient. I told myself not to settle for anything less than a mature buck, a four-point with antlers wider than his ears.

Every few steps opened to a different perspective. Using binoculars, I looked into every canyon and washout and explored the shadows of the junipers and rocky outcroppings.

From the map I knew there was a spring on the western side of the ridge. Cautious, I glassed beneath the trees. If the spring waters continued through September, there would be animals closeby. There was. Cattle. A black angus stood in the muddy water. I moved up the hill and out of the draw.

The buck's body was half in light, half in shadow as he fed across the hogback toward a morning bed on the shaded west slope. I watched through binoculars. Catching movement, he turned his head to look and showed me a glimpse of polished antlers wider than the tips of his ears. I counted four points on each side.

I waited. It was his move. I didn't want to take the shot without a rest. He put his head down to take another mouthful of sage.

I moved, tipping my hat off and shrugging out of my backpack. There was one juniper between us. A low-hanging bough provided a good rest. I snugged the rifle into my shoulder and thumbed the safety forward, finding the buck in the crosshairs.

He turned toward me, head down, his gray coat sleek from a summer of good feed, sunlight on his grizzled face and antlers. I felt the recoil in my shoulder and heard the echo ring out across the valley. I admired this animal of the juniper and sage, thankful for the meat and for the trophy. I looked out across the tops of the hills—north, south, east, and west.

I often pursue bucks by myself because it is hard to find a partner who wants to travel to a different spot each year. Going solo allows me to focus on the hunt. As much as I loved the solitude, I suddenly realized there was a lot of meat that must be packed

Cody Waldo with a fantastic mule deer he took while hunting desert country. Pre-season scouting helped him locate this buck. Photo courtesy Ray Waldo.

out, skinned, cut and put in the cooler. And only one man to do it.

It was after dark when I finally took a swim and sipped some hot chocolate. The stars were bright. There was wind in the treetops again. Simple pleasures. 🌿

There is a satisfaction that the hunter knows when he realizes his goal. That satisfaction is magnified when the hunt ends early on opening day.

To ensure early season success, spend the months prior to your hunt studying maps and talking to people who have hunted your area extensively.

Pick five good areas and buy topographical maps for each location. Look for travel routes: saddles, benches, and river bottoms. Look for edge habitat that will provide food and cover. Because opening day often arrives ahead of the rain, look for water.

Heavy bedding cover can double as feed. Broad-leaf plants and browse are the best bets. Deer want bedding areas that will allow them to see and/or hear danger. You have to play their game to find them. You have to be quiet—one misstep can blow months of planning. Be sure to have the wind in your face, or risk running the deer out of the pocket before you get there.

Study aerial photos for detail you won't find on a map. Look for large rock piles or outcroppings that force animals to detour. These can be great places to find game because traveling deer have to find a way around them. Look for small ponds or greenery that might indicate a spring. Look for ledges that might shelter a sleeping buck.

MY FRIEND DOUG SCRIBNER found his buck in similar terrain that year. His basin was choked with tall sage. A lone juniper nearly 800 yards away provided the only shade against the coming sun. Doug and his partner, George Baldini, moved into position, jumping a three-point and a twenty-inch four-point in the process.

They watched from a high vantage point, employing spotting scope and ten-power binoculars. As the sun came up, they scanned the finger ridges. A half-dozen does were scattered around the lonely juniper. Another deer had his head behind the trunk. George focused the scope and waited for the animal to raise his head.

Sunlight glinted on antlers. George whispered, "He's a keeper."

The deer was in the steepest part of the draw, and Doug would have to make it past six pairs of female eyes in order to get close enough to the buck for a good shot. Using the tree as a landmark he made his way down the hill, moving slowly through the sage.

The deer was lying down but Doug could see antler tips as he moved in. Nervous, the animal tested the air with his nose, turned his ears and looked around. Then he saw Doug and in an instant was running.

Doug's 270 Winchester went to his shoulder, he found the moving animal in the scope and squeezed as the reticle crossed the vitals.

He crossed the stony ground to examine the magnificent animal he had taken. A 29-inch non-typical muley.

Doug believes there is no substitute for knowing the area that you are hunting. Fortunate enough to draw the coveted tags two years in a row, Doug had done his scouting and was well aware of the potential to take a big-antlered mule deer from this basin. One year he hunted for nine days and spotted 52 bucks—including some in the 30-inch range—before taking an animal. He came to know his area well. On opening day the following year, he knew exactly where to go and what to do.

In big country, Doug lets his knowledge of the terrain and his optics cover the ground for him. 🦌

A FEW MILES AWAY, Southeast Oregon hunters Cody and Ray Waldo, employed similar tactics to help fourteen year-old Cody bag the biggest muley of his life.

Cody and his dad, Ray, first heard about the big buck from bass fishermen during the summer. He was a big four-point, they said. The Waldos were to find out just *how* big....

During archery season they were able to get close— stalking to within fifteen

Dave Hamilton watches a mountain trail from a rocky ledge. Deer and other game are forced to detour around large rocks like this one. Such places can give a hunter a good stand. Gary Lewis photo.

yards. Cody ran the video camera while a close friend tried to make the shot. The arrow missed the mark but the film and the photos helped inspire Cody and Ray for the coming rifle season.

Early on opening morning, they found the gray monarch again. Ray had a shot, but the buck gave him just a fleeting glimpse. Disappointed, father and son returned to the fundamentals of hunting desert deer— watching, glassing, and waiting.

Two hours later, scanning the far canyon wall through his spotting scope, Cody spotted the buck bedded in the shadow of high rimrock.

This time it was Cody's turn. The stalk took an hour and a half as he picked his way down a side draw and up another. Hidden from the muley's view on the rim above the animal, he carefully worked into position and readied the borrowed rifle—his mom's 6mm Remington. He looked over the edge and, at fifteen yards, made his shot.

For Cody, the season was over and the work began. Ray backed up and took pictures of his son's trophy, then they measured the antler spread. The big four-point taped 32 inches wide with a tiny chip missing from the tip of one tine.

The Waldos credit their success to having knowledge of the buck's habits and territory. Patience, a spotting scope, a long stalk, and a well-placed shot rewarded father and son with a memory that will last their lifetimes. 🌿

Hunters who employ optics for open-country mule deer know that spot-and-stalk deer hunting produces larger bucks for the least amount of work.

Look for places where you can get into position without being seen. Be there before first light, slip over the crest of a hill, or through a stand of trees. Don't watch into the sun. Stay downwind.

Set your tripod so that you will be in a comfortable position you can maintain for a long time. Carry a small pad to sit on or fold up a shirt to smooth out the bumps on the ground.

Although they spooked the buck early and were unable to make the first shot, the Waldos were patient, systematically scanning possible hiding places. They used a viewing system that divides the ground they are watching into quadrants, scanning each quadrant until satisfied that they had seen everything.

Spotting at sunrise is best; but deer can be found feeding until ten o'clock in the morning and sometimes longer on cloudy days. Hunt all day. As Cody Waldo proved, bedded deer can also be spotted. Look for parts of a deer. The shine of a wet nose, an antler tine, the flick of an ear, the crook of a back leg, or the horizontal line of a back can give away the hiding spot of your next trophy mule deer.

Once you find a buck you want to pursue, look just as hard to see if there are any animals nearby that might spoil your stalk. Not only will you have to keep out of sight of the deer you're after, you will need to detour around the lesser animal that he is using as his first line of defense.

The rimrock, sage, and juniper of our western plains hide mule deer monarchs that most hunters only dream about. Take the time to learn your area before the hunt and make good use of optics in open country. Your dream of a monster muley may become reality.

WHERE TO HUNT FOR BLACKTAILS

You will have different challenges to find the best habitat and hunting grounds for blacktails.

The key is to find pockets of public-access ground surrounded by private land or to hunt beyond road-closure barriers.

One season we hunted Oregon's Alsea Unit

Ryan Eicher sets a waypoint before leaving the parking area on a morning hunt in the mountains of Central Oregon.

for blacktails. Parking at a locked a gate outside of timber company land, we found the deer a mile in. It was Saturday and we were within a forty-minute drive of a major city, but we saw no other hunters.

Blacktail deer thrive in logged areas. The bow hunter does well when concentrating on travel routes leading to and from recent timber harvests. Because of the diversity of feed, deer are also abundant near farms and plantations. The catch is that public access is more difficult. Do not hunt on private land unless you have prior permission.

The blacktail breeding season usually begins in the second week of November so the late-season hunter has an advantage. During that time does are distracted and bucks lose a little of their wariness.

In good habitat, use your binoculars more than your boots. If you are

The road is closed to motorized vehicles. Is it an obstacle or an opportunity? The choice is up to you. Gary Lewis photo.

looking for antlers, keep track of the does. A buck may be close by. Watch for parts of the deer. Often, just an antler tip, a wet nose, an eye, an ear, or a tail is what you will see first. Look for the horizontal line of a back or the crook of a rear leg against a vertical forest.

One- to five-year-old clearcuts provide good feed for blacktails. But don't expect to find big deer out in the open during the day. Instead, watch the fringes and the small openings.

Examine aerial photos and topo maps to find the places where bucks hide. Locate roadless areas and natural escape routes such as saddles and canyons. Look for brushy shelves where a deer can watch his backtrail from his bed.

Where are you going to hunt? A good bet for high numbers of blacktails might be in pockets of public land surrounded by private holdings. To find these look at BLM or National Forest Service Maps. Find the area of the unit that you want to hunt then narrow it down with a good topographical map such as the USGS 7.5 minute series. These maps are usually eight square miles, show topo lines, most backroads, and some trails. Choose an area where various types of habitat converge. Select several potential spots then consult aerial photos. Look for farmland, streams, and foothills, paying special attention to areas of recent logging activity.

Though deer densities can go as high as 150 per square mile, this isn't easy hunting. Scent control is everything. Hunt into the wind. Generally, blacktails move downhill to feed in the evening, uphill toward bed in the morning. Glass high slopes and clearcuts before noon and look for bedding areas at midday. Still-hunt well-used trails in the afternoon and stay out until dark. The best chance of seeing a buck is during the last five minutes of shooting light.

Watch for well-used travel lanes from bedding to feeding areas. In the foothills, pay particular attention to wooded finger ridges where deer can travel out of sight. Often deer seen from a distance can be ambushed with a little hurried planning.

The blacktail rut usually begins about the middle of November and will loosen up the more wary animals. That will be your best opportunity to find deer during the day. Try rattling horns, fawn calls, and grunt calls—but give them time to work and more than just a token effort.

ACCESSING THE BEST HUNTING BY MOUNTAIN BIKE

When I began to go on hunting trips with my Dad, and later with an uncle and cousin, we drove any road we wanted to, parked where we wished, and hiked from there.

That was then, and quite frankly, we saw less game in those days. Forest road closures have changed all that. And the face of hunting is changing. On the negative side, many hunters don't have access to all hunting areas. On the positive side, deer and elk are less harried. The more distance a hunter can put between himself and a traveled road, the more game he is likely to see.

One way to quickly cover a lot of ground is on a mountain bike. It may not be standard hunting equipment for most hunters but many people are finding out just how useful they can be.

A properly equipped mountain bike can carry your water and food, your weapon, tent, and sleeping-bag—even the game you harvest.

My bike is made by ZLC, has a carbon fiber frame, wide pedals to hold the tread of my hunting boots, 27 hill-climbing speeds, knobby tires, fenders, and a rifle rack.

The first thing you need is a way to carry your bow, shotgun or rifle. Racks are mounted to your handlebars and can be purchased at bike shops and sporting goods stores.

Next is a way to carry extra gear. A rack mounted behind the seat is a handy place for game bags, rope, and lunch. A water bottle mounted to the frame can be a lifesaver on a hot day. Another necessary piece of equipment is a lock and chain. This will ensure the bike will still be there at the end of the day and not be pedaled down the trail by some boot-weary hiker.

Be sure you have a headlamp or battery-powered lamp mounted up front to light your way on moonless nights. A helmet is also a good idea because the weight distribution on a bike is different with extra gear, so chances of a spill are increased.

At first glance, a closed road is an inconvenience. You need to find a new place to hunt or figure out a different mode of transportation. A closed road is simply a new challenge, an opportunity.

The mountain bike is a way to travel farther and faster than your boot-sore brethren. Properly outfitted, your bike can carry you far from the blaze-orange horde and well-traveled roads to the high-country meadows and thickets where deer and elk are less pressured and the hunting opportunity can be fantastic.

Gary Lewis on his mountain bike. It carries his lunch, a camera, an extra water bottle and his rifle. Gary Lewis photo.

PACKING IN

I ONCE BACK-PACKED into the Snake River canyon with two friends, hunting for spring black bear. We crossed the river and carried camp on our backs for a two-hour hike up a rocky canyon, staying "in the bush" for three days. We ate fish, jerky, dried fruit, and energy bars. We took our water from a creek, pumping it through a purifier.

Every morning we woke with the sunlight bringing new life to the wildflowers and color to the lichen-encrusted canyon walls.

At the end of the stay, we picked our way back along a cliff trail, through rattlesnakes and—as we figured out later—poison oak. We left behind a lucky bear, fifteen bighorn rams, chukar, and the mule deer that we watched from camp.

I was satisfied. Not with the food or my shooting, but with three good days spent in the wild, away from traffic, telephones, and television.

Memories like these provide balance against life in the city. As I look back over the camping, hunting and fishing trips I have made in the last ten years, the ones that stand out are the trips into the backcountry. 🦌

The items in your pack must be included with good reason. Every extra ounce makes a difference after two hours carrying it on the trail.

If you will be traveling any distance at all, your choice of pack represents the most critical decision. It should not be purchased through the mail. You need to try several different models until you find the right fit.

My pack is made by Vortex. It fits me like a well-used deerskin glove. It carries the weight low on my back so that I'm not inclined to topple while crossing a creek or a slide. With tent, sleeping bag, and pad removed, it can double as a day-pack to carry camera, water, and lunch.

Next in importance is your sleeping bag. Whether you choose down or synthetic, pick a bag that will protect you against the extremes of weather you are likely to encounter. Down bags are generally less bulky than synthetic, but down loses its insulating ability when wet.

A sleeping pad is important. You may be tempted to go without a pad to save the added weight a pad adds to your pack, but that extra bit of comfort

Gary Lewis holds the gate open on the road out from hunting camp. Leave all gates the way you found them. Gary Lewis photo.

may be what makes the difference between a trip to remember and a trip to forget. I use a self-inflating Camp Mat.

A tent (or tarp) is necessary in the high country where snow can fall during any month of the year. Tents are also a good way to keep bugs at arm's length in the evening.

One oft-forgotten item is a water filter. Very little of the water found in the wilderness is safe to drink. You cannot pack in enough water to keep you hydrated on a trip lasting more than a couple of days.

The purifier Dan brought on our Snake River trip gave the water a pronounced foul flavor. By the second day, I would have given $10.00 for a packet of Tang to mix it with. But as bad as it tasted we didn't get sick.

The Bottom's Up water filtration bottle has worked well for me. I use their 18-ounce model. It fits easily inside my pack—out of the way until needed.

A backpacker's stove is optional because you can get all the nourishment you need from canned and pre-packaged foods. But there is something civilized and reassuring about a cup of soup at lunch or a cup of hot chocolate at the end of an evening.

If you want a taste of civilization in the wilderness, try one of the "Self-Heating" meals. Pull the string, wait 20 minutes while it cooks itself, and eat. Utensils, salt, pepper, napkin, and tray are all included. The only thing missing is a waiter to bring it to you.

If poison oak grows where you hunt, consider carrying Tecnu Oak-N-Ivy brand outdoor skin cleanser. A quick wash with this soap will keep you from coming down with a terrible rash if you find yourself in a patch of poison oak.

Whether you will be pursuing game with rifle, bow, or camera will determine what else you bring. The one thing you shouldn't bring with you is the frantic pace of daily life! The world would be a much saner place if everyone could know what its like to watch the world awaken from a wilderness camp, the sun bringing life to a new day.

Gary Lewis with an opening day 4-point he took on the edge of a treeless plain.

Chapter 5

WHERE DEER LIVE

REMEMBER IDENTIFYING deer tracks as a nine-year-old boy. We were a party of about six, hunting in the Coal Creek area of Southwest Washington. I was along to learn that the *non-hunters* always see the big bucks, how *not* to shoot, and how *not* to step in a bee hive.

I walked with my dad. The trail led along the ridge top and out through some reprod. We met some other hunters at the end of it. A tall one carrying a .30-06 and a short one carrying a .30-30—a good "brush gun," he called it (the first time I had heard those words). "Seen anything?" they asked.

Yes, I had seen two massive blacktails fighting over a doe. I had seen a flustered hunter jam his rifle trying to shoot one of the bucks. I hadn't stepped on the beehive yet—that would come later. But you don't tell other hunters those things. You want them to think there aren't any bucks around.

Dad said, "Not much."

I looked down at the ground. "Look at all these fresh deer tracks."

The short one then uttered those famous words I've heard hundreds of times since. "You can't eat tracks, boy."

Maybe you can't eat tracks, but somewhere there is a deer stepping out of tracks just like those. And you *can* eat him!

What can tracks tell you? What should a deer hunter know about tracking? How will understanding tracks make you a better hunter?

First of all, the presence of tracks indicates that at some point a deer occupied the place you now stand. That's good news, because just maybe, that deer is still close by.

Unless there's snow on the ground and the sign is fresh, you may not be able to track a buck in order to make a shot. However, the tracks can give you clues to where the deer bed, what they are feeding on, and where they take their water.

Spend a day following tracks, observing tracks, and finding where they lead. To determine where animals are bedding, backtrack the fresh prints you find in the evening If you lose the trail, make wide circles until you find them again.

Bring a tape measure and note the length and width of the hooves. You'll notice that some hooves are sharp-pointed while others are chipped and dull. With practice you'll be able to differentiate between tracks and find the track of an individual animal.

Tracks also give the hunter an idea about the size and sex of the animals in an area. Bucks are bigger than does. They have longer legs, wider bodies, and make longer strides. Their track will be fuller than a smaller deer, and sometimes—due to body weight—a track will appear splayed.

A doe's front shoulders and hindquarters are similar in width, so on flat ground a doe's back feet will fall in the same line as her front feet. An older buck's chest is wider than his hindquarters, so his back hoofprints are found inside his front prints. Dewclaws are more apt to be found in the tracks of a big buck.

Mature buck deer also have longer tracks than does. Mature blacktail bucks leave a track that measures almost 3-1/4 inches in length.

Carry something to measure tracks with while hunting. For the past few seasons, I have been hunting with a 7mm Magnum. Coincidentally, the factory-loaded Federal Premium 160-grain Nosler Partition bullets I use measure just under 3-1/4 inches. If a bullet is the same length as the track, I know I am in the presence of blacktail-greatness.

My biggest mule deer buck had hooves that measured 3-1/2 inches long and left tracks that were splayed with the weight of his body.

Big mule deer tracks will vary dependent on local conditions. Body sizes vary somewhat across mule deer range. But by paying attention to tracks you can tell the approximate sizes of the deer where you hunt.

In one unit I like to hunt in Eastern Oregon, I have found that a three-and-a-half year old three-point muley will leave tracks that measure three inches. A buck this size is usually bigger in body than the average doe. It would be safe to say that any three inch or longer track in that area was made by a buck.

BEDS

In most conditions deer will bed on any side of a hill, but in extreme weather you will find them in greater concentrations on one particular side.

In hot weather, look on north-facing slopes where shadows are longest during midday. In cold weather, pay more attention to south-facing slopes where deer can find the sun lingering longer.

Where would your buck bed? Look to the shade—up against a rock wall or under a tree where he would find some relief in the afternoon. It would be a place where he could see other deer and also observe predators. It would be a high place with at least two escape routes because no wild animal wants to be trapped.

If the weather is hot and dry, think about where the nearest water is. If the deer have to go a long way downhill for water, they will bed lower on the slope so they don't have to travel as far.

On a hogback, deer might bed where they can slip over the hill in either

Jodi Applegate with a super buck she took late in the season. Patience, persistence, and a well-placed shot paid off. Photo courtesy Applegate family.

direction to evade predators. Look for a clearing where deer can watch for approaching danger. They will bed on the upwind side so they can smell danger from behind as they watch the clearing.

In high winds, deer will bed in the lee of anything that will protect them from the storm. Look in sheltered hollows, on benches on the downwind side of ridges, and in steep draws. Deer don't like high wind. Don't waste your time hunting where the deer aren't.

BIG BUCKS OFTEN USE smaller deer as sacrificial decoys. Once, on a scouting trip, we hiked to the top of a ridge and watched for bucks. I was happy to find so many animals in the area I had picked from a map, but just a little concerned that I had found no tracks bigger than those made by some average three-points. Were there any bigger bucks in the area?

We walked along below the shoulder of the ridge in the hot August sun. Suddenly, a deer leaped from its bed on the northeast side of a tall juniper. I

Dave Hamilton sets up along a trail, using camouflage, and a fallen tree for cover. Gary Lewis photo.

swung up my binoculars and locked on his head. He was a buck sporting four-inch spikes. He pounded away up the hill and doubled back, giving us a good look at him from the side. We kept walking in the direction we'd been heading, and finally the big buck could take it no longer. He sprang from his bed—putting a stand of junipers between us—and pounded downhill across the open basin. I didn't need binoculars to see how big he was. His antlers were far wider than the tips of his ears or the girth of his middle. He was at least a 34-inch muley with four points on the left and five on the right. At 350 yards away, he stopped and looked back at us, then he pogo-sticked over the top of a small hill and went out of sight.

That buck had used the spike as a decoy. Had it been rifle season, the smaller buck that ran uphill might have taken a bullet and the bigger buck would have made his escape to the desert. I wondered how many other deer that wise old buck had sacrificed over the years. It was interesting that the deer went the opposite direction the spike had taken. His plan was to put distance between himself and the hunter. He headed away from the junipers and the patch of mountain mahogany that could have hidden him, straight out to the open desert flats.

Spending the rest of the season beneath one of those lone junipers he would be safe with visibility of hundreds of yards in every direction. 🌵

ANOTHER TIME I was bowhunting for elk in Oregon's Ochocos when I paused to rest beside a spring. It was a warm day and I liked the shade that I found on the edge of the thick timber overlooking a large meadow below me. I wasn't the only one who liked the coolness of that spot on a hot day. A small buck was bedded only a few yards away. He leaped from his bed like he'd been launched from a slingshot. Running a little way, he stopped to look at me when I blew on my cow call. Suddenly another deer was up and running without pausing to look behind him. I didn't get a look at his antlers but I saw by the size of his body that he was a much bigger deer. I believe he hooked that smaller buck in the rear end, encouraging him to run uphill while he made his escape downhill.

On the same hunt, I jumped another deer from his bed while still-hunting along a ridge. He was a forked-horn buck who had chosen his hiding place with a lack of foresight that would have earned him a quick trip to the meat locker if I had possessed a deer tag.

From his vantage, he could watch a great clearcut that was below him. Danger could not approach from below without him seeing it. But he'd neglected to think about the trail at his back. Maybe he will pick his bed a little better next time. 🌵

You can identify a deer's sex by looking at the bed it left behind. A urine spot in the center of the bed indicates a buck rested there. Urine spots on the edge indicate a doe used the bed.

DIET

A typical mule deer's diet consists of 55% browse (the new growth of trees, shrubs, and vines with woody stems), 22% forbs (broadleaf plants), 10% grasses, 7% nuts, and 6% other materials (Pious Report, 1989). Typical browse plants in mule deer country are sagebrush and bitterbrush.

Curlleaf Cercocarpus is another important mule deer food. Also called mountain mahogany, this shrub/tree is found from Southeast Washington to Montana and south to Southern California and Northern Arizona. You

A typical mule deer diet consists of 55% browse material. Typical browse plants in mule deer country are sagebrush and bitterbrush. Gary Lewis photo.

will find it on mountain slopes from elevations of 4,000 to 10,500 feet. Elk, deer, and antelope make good use of these stands of trees all year long, both as cover and feed.

Browse is abundant in mule deer habitat, but broadleaf plants are mule deer favorites. Locate these plants, confirm the deer are eating

Broadleaf plants make up over 20% of a mule deer's diet. Locate these plants, confirm deer are eating them and spend time watching in the morning and evening. Gary Lewis photo.

them and spend time watching in the morning and evening.

That forked horn that I bounced from his bed on the ridge trotted out into the three-year old clearcut and stopped about 150 yards away—another fatal error, had I been carrying a rifle. As I watched him, it occurred to me that there might be other deer feeding in the same area. I sat down and watched and saw nothing besides about ten head of cattle, feeding on bunchgrass.

Then I picked up my binoculars and spotted a doe, and then another. They were deer I couldn't pick out among the young pines and manzanita with my naked eye.

TELLING BUCKS FROM DOES AT A DISTANCE

There are few hunting situations where the hunter is allowed to take a deer of either sex. For this reason, the hunter needs to be very sure of the target before pulling the trigger.

An old hunter once told me with unfailing certainty that he could tell bucks from does simply by observing their body language. Bucks, he said, move and act differently than does. He was right. By learning to tell the differences you can quickly look over a group of deer and pick the bucks from the does or pick out does from among a group of bucks.

Before you read any further, understand that I do not advocate making shooting decisions based on body language. Shots should be taken only after the hunter has determined that the target animal is a legal animal by verifying the presence or absence of antlers.

FREQUENTLY, BUCKS SPAR among themselves to establish and maintain dominance in a herd.

Once I watched a group of thirty deer moving out of a little sagebrush basin. The deer were far away, but I had noticed a forkhorn and a four-point in the group. However, with all the animals moving together, I was unable to focus on a legal animal through the spotting scope and call it out to my partner. I watched, finally picking out two deer on the far right of the herd. The deer on the left, bigger through the shoulders than the one on the right, stopped to swing his head down low in the direction of the smaller deer. The two deer put their heads together. I zoomed in, saw antlers and called the shot.

"See the two deer on the right of the herd? Take the one on the left," I said. The big gun spoke and, as I watched through the scope, I saw a puff of dirt give evidence of the miss. The deer trotted over a rise and out of sight. 🌿

Once they reach two and a half years of age, bucks begin to grow larger than their sisters. Males get blocky looking with big shoulders. Their front legs are farther apart than their rear legs and they walk with a jaunty attitude that ripples the muscles beneath their gray hair. Does move with more graceful steps, placing their hooves in the same line.

Bucks will also sniff at the tails of does. If you see two deer traveling together, the buck will almost always bring up the rear. This is done for security and breeding purposes, both high priorities of big muleys.

If deer are feeding in a group, a dominant buck often stands just a little apart from the others. Similarly, if a lone doe accompanies a group of bucks, the doe may feed just a little apart.

Spend time watching deer and note the actions and characteristics of the deer you see. Practice guessing the sex of the deer you see from a distance, then look at them through binoculars or spotting scope. In time, you may learn to distinguish a buck from a doe before confirming it by seeing antlers.

BINOCULARS

Good binoculars are a necessity for any hunter who wants to tie a tag on a deer. Hang them on a comfortable strap from your neck with an elastic strap that holds them to your body so they don't flop uncomfortably against your chest. You need to have quick access and use them often. They must be waterproof if you will hunt in the rain and snow. Don't leave them in a case. Don't carry them in a backpack. After your weapon and knife, your binoculars are the most important tool you can use on a deer hunt.

Save your compact binoculars for watching ball games and concerts. When a deer or antelope is your goal, don't skimp. Carry the best full-size binoculars you can afford. Compact binoculars just don't give you the brightness and resolution you need during those critical best times to hunt—early morning and late evening.

I USED TO CARRY a compact binocular which couldn't even do the job in mid-morning. It's easy to cover a lot of territory early in the archery season. So in the interest of saving weight, I was carrying a lightweight folding binocular that fit nicely into the pocket of my camouflage shirt.

The small green meadows were strung together like emeralds in a jeweled necklace. We walked the edges, watching the shadows for feeding elk. We looked into basins and glassed islands of timber for browsing deer. Then, Ryan spotted them—two deer feeding as they walked.

They were out about a hundred yards, moving through the timber feeding on mushrooms and tender new growth. Studying the animals intently through the binoculars I handed him, Ryan couldn't make out whether or not they had antlers. We followed, trying to anticipate their moves. Slowly they put distance between us and were soon lost to view, still unaware of our presence.

Following them took us away from the lush bowls of green grass and into the tinder-dry woods. We ghosted along, stopping frequently to look for deer.

Primos Pro-Staffer Walt Ramage with a Wyoming mule deer he took on a recent hunt. Photo courtesy Walt Ramage.

In a dry creek bed a lone deer fed head down. It was eighty yards away and I lifted my binoculars. "Buck or doe?" Ryan asked.

"No antlers," I reported. We picked our way using bushes and trees as cover. When we were within thirty yards I could see that the deer was clearly a buck. He had six-inch spikes atop his head. That day I realized I was using the wrong binoculars. If my 8x21 compacts couldn't render antlers on a deer then I needed something better. 🌿

The choice of optics almost always represents a compromise. You want quality, you pay more money. You want more magnification, you carry heavier glasses. If you can't afford top quality and you don't want to carry bulky glasses, you buy something smaller and more affordable. It's a compromise. Fortunately, there are a lot of good quality optics to choose from.

For all-around use, 7x to 10x are probably the best choice. Higher magnifications reduce field-of-view necessary for locating game. And with higher magnification, movements of the hands are magnified. For this reason I prefer 7x and 8x.

The second factor to consider is brightness. Brightness is what determines the ability to see detail through the lenses, (especially in low light). Hold your binoculars twelve inches from your eyes and look through the eyepiece. What you see is a small point of light called the exit pupil. For maximum brightness the exit pupil should be as large as the pupil in your eye. The human pupil can dilate to a maximum of five millimeters in low light so to deliver maximum brightness the exit pupil in your binoculars should be the same.

To arrive at exit pupil size, just divide the magnification into the size of the objective lens. For example, 8 into 40 equals an exit pupil of five times the size of your dilated eye. Divide 8 into 21 and you get 2 and 5/8— a big reduction in brightness.

The best binoculars for the hunter are those that come the closest to fulfilling the need for clarity, brightness, magnification, and weight. The best choice probably compromises one or more elements, but you'll never regret buying quality.

SPOTTING SCOPES

In that magical hour before first light, I slip into place and set up the tripod, affixing my spotting scope. Wind direction is always considered first. If my scent is blowing toward the place I expect to see deer, I find

Gary Lewis studies a group of mule deer through a spotting scope. Long-range viewing can save a lot of walking in open country. Gary Lewis photo.

another place to hunt for the morning, *or* another angle to watch from.

Before using the scope, thoroughly scan the area with your binoculars. Start with the closest ground first, working farther out. With the wider field of view afforded by the binos, you may spot the deer faster than with the scope.

After scanning with the binoculars, take a seat behind the scope and go to work. Use a systematic search. First, identify the most likely spots to find feeding deer. Look in each spot in turn. Second, break up the landscape into a grid and begin a sector-by-sector search. Again, look at the closest ground first. With your scope set at its lowest setting, start on the lower left. Focus the scope to bring the foliage into clarity. Don't touch the tripod. Simply look, taking in the shape, the color and the texture of the habitat. Look for parts of the deer or for something out of place. When you have exhausted your circular view of the country, turn the scope to the right to carefully examine the next view.

Work your grid a piece at a time from left to right, from the bottom of the screen to the horizon. When finished, start again. As the morning comes on, the sun will illuminate more of the ground. Shadows will change in shape and expose different views. Sometimes a deer will feed out from behind a grove of trees. Maybe you missed him the first time, but you might spot him the second time through.

When you see a deer you want to pursue, take a long careful look around him to determine whether there are any other deer close by. In the case of a large buck, there is usually a smaller deer near, acting as bodyguard.

A good spotting scope is one that renders distant objects with clarity and brightness of color. It will not give the viewer a headache after ten minutes of use. Like all optics, the spotting scope reflects a compromise between weight, clarity, brightness, magnification and price.

Don't hurry into buying a scope. Compare several models side by side—outdoors if possible. Set up the scopes on tripods to view a far-off sign or a business card placed at some distance. Throw out the scopes that don't render the print clearly, then look for brightness of color. Here's where quality shines through.

Next, look at durability and ruggedness. Where I hunt, waterproofing is very important and so is rubber armoring. If I drop my scope in the rocks, I want to know there's a reasonable chance that I will still be able to use it later in the day. This brings up another point. If you break your scope, will the manufacturer replace it? A good warranty can be another reason to pick between two otherwise similar scopes.

My scope is a Wind River 15-45x60mm model. It is waterproof, rubber-armored and easy on my eye. It represented the best compromise I could find in a spotting scope at the time. I compared it to several other models and found it a good value within my price range.

RANGE FINDERS

These days, many deer hunters are carrying laser rangefinders. A rangefinder can help the hunter measure the distance to the animal prior to the shot. Confident of the range, a hunter who recognizes the limitations of his equipment can stalk into range and take his best shot.

The laser rangefinder is a range-measuring unit with the capability of instantly measuring distances. It works with laser technology, emitting a pulse of laser light to a reflective target (if the deer's body is concealed by a tree, you can focus on something nearby). The laser flight time is measured as the reflection is received in the rangefinder. Calculation is instantaneous and the distance is displayed on the rangefinder's liquid crystal display.

Rangefinders are usually equipped with 2x to 8x optics allowing monocular or binocular viewing.

Several manufacturers offer quality laser rangefinders, but not all are created equal. Again, make an informed decision before spending your hard-earned money. Archers have different requirements than rifle hunters. If bow and arrow is your bag, you'll want a model that has a minimum range of at least five or ten yards. Rifle hunters should be more concerned with the maximum range the rangefinder is capable of.

For the rifle hunter, the upper limit of the rangefinder should be approximately 700 yards or better. Most rifles are not capable of taking game at that distance, but if your effective range is 200 yards, you can quickly calculate how many yards you must stalk before setting up for a shot.

Weather, visibility, and reflectance have an impact on the actual distance your rangefinder can calculate. All of these factors should be taken into account before selecting a rangefinder.

One of the most popular models is a product from Bushnell called the Yardage Pro Legend. Waterproof, it weighs only seven ounces and is small enough to fit into a pocket. Its vertical design makes for easy, one-handed use. It is accurate from 10 yards to a maximum 930 yards. It's as simple to use as finding the deer in the crosshair and pressing a button. The range is calculated and displayed instantaneously. (When I tested it I tracked a moving animal at 68 yards. The deer moved to within 40 yards and turned away.)

Nate Simmons used a 7mm Magnum to take this nice buck on an October, 2001 hunt in Idaho's Hells Canyon. Photo courtesy Nate Simmons.

Dave Hamilton on an eastern Oregon bowhunt. In this photo he is wearing four different types of camouflage. Pick a pattern (or patterns) that will blend into the habitat you will be hunting. Choose one that remains visibly broken at distances beyond 50 yards. Gary Lewis photo.

Chapter 6

SIGHT,
SOUND, AND SMELL

Hunting Deer Where They Live

To successfully hunt deer in the pockets where they eat, sleep, recreate and procreate, you must beat the senses they employ to protect themselves from predators. Every day, deer rely upon their eyes, their ears, and their noses to alert them to danger. They are far better at staying alive than we are at turning them into venison steaks.

Most hunters know that it's better to see the animal before it sees us. In fact, if such a thing were possible, we would find that far more deer see us than we are aware of. *Then how do we beat their vision and see them before they see us?* The key is to understand how deer *see.*

Deer are not color-blind as many of us once thought. Scientists now believe that deer see in shades of gray, blue, and yellow. The colors yellow, orange, red, and brown are seen as shades of yellow. A deer's eyes are sensitive to ultraviolet light, especially in low light conditions. Researchers believe ultra-violet light is seen through a deer's eyes as a bright bluish glow. The thoughtful hunter will realize that wearing blue jeans or a blue denim jacket while hunting for big game is not a good idea.

Most home laundry detergents contain ultraviolet brighteners that make the colors of our clothes appealing to the human eye. The trouble is that these color enhancers make us more visible to deer. if you want to help keep deer from spotting you, wash your clothes in the river or use a detergent that contains no brighteners. A product called Sport-Wash is a detergent that uses no artificial brighteners. It is available through archery shops and mail order. U-V-Killer is a spray-on product that neutralizes UV brighteners in fabric.

Camouflaged clothing is helpful. Wear a pattern that will blend into the natural surroundings where you hunt. Before you buy, look at the pattern you are considering from a distance. Does it all blend together when viewed from afar, or does it appear random and broken? You want a pattern that appears broken, that doesn't go all black or all green or all brown when viewed from 50 yards away.

For safety reasons, I believe a hunter should wear high visibility hunter-orange when hunting during firearm seasons. But the rifle hunter has options that will make him or her less visible to deer. Wearing a hunter orange hat is a good compromise many hunters make for safety. A checkered shirt or jacket can also provide the broken pattern that will keep you from standing out to the eyes of a deer.

Avoid colors that might cause you to be mistaken for game. (Once I was watching a clearcut for elk. I spotted movement at the tree line 300 yards away. I lifted my binoculars and made out the front legs and torso of an elk. As I steadied the glasses, I could see that the elk was a man dressed in black pants and a buckskin-colored jacket.) Leave your blacks, grays, whites, and buckskin colors at home during deer and elk season. Wear greens, browns, tans, and plaids that blend with your surroundings. Wear some hunter orange in firearms seasons.

Since a deer's vision is tuned to pick up movement, keep the movements of your hands to a minimum. Your extremities are subject to the most movement.

Traditional archer William Roberts with a nice 4-point mule deer he tagged on a hunt in Nevada's Ruby Mountains. William Roberts photo.

Don't wear hunter orange on your arms, hands, or legs. Don't dress them up in flashy colors. Reduce the shine of your face by using face paint, a mask, or a beard. In warm weather, wear mosquito net gloves to keep your hands from betraying you. In a buck's core area, when you move, move slow.

SOUND

I have hunted with people who make a lot of noise in deer country. Some people are just heavy walkers. I have hunted with others who make very little noise, moving as quietly as a light breeze. The quiet ones kill more deer.

Starting with the drive into the hunt area, turn off the music and don't race the engine. When you park, set the emergency brake quietly. Don't slam the door or the trunk or tailgate. Push it closed and lean against it until it clicks shut.

Deer pay attention to anything that sounds foreign to their ears. If they learn to associate the sound of an approaching vehicle with the two-legged predators that sling arrows at them, you'll have to work harder to tie your tag around their antlers.

Believe it or not, I know people who wear earplugs hunting so that the sound of a shot won't hurt their ears. Earplugs minimize their chances of killing deer because hearing is an important sense we can use to help us locate deer. Earplugs will also lull you into thinking that you are not making any noise as you walk. If *you* can't hear the sound of the branch you just stepped on, you won't think about the deer hearing it. Deer stay alive by paying attention to little sounds like that. Better to put earplugs in right before making the shot.

Remember, if you startle one deer and it warns another deer that danger is near, you probably won't get a chance at either animal.

In dry weather, it is better to stay out of some areas until first light just because it's hard to move wtihout making noise.

Wear boots or sneaking shoes that allow you to feel the branches beneath your feet. (One successful bowhunter I know hunts only in socks.) Pick your

Moccasins or soft overshoes such as these Baer's Feet, can help you make your stalk with less noise. Gary Lewis photo.

way around downed branches instead of trying to walk through them. Be conscious of the sound of your footfall. Be quiet.

Sounds can also alert *you* to the presence of deer. Mule deer, blacktail, whitetails, and axis deer can be heard vocalizing. I have heard blacktail deer feeding in heavy brush, calling to each other with a sound that I characterize as "huck-huck." The deer were relaxed. The sounds seemed contented, a way of telling the other deer that they were close by. Fawns can sometimes be heard bleating when they are separated from their mother. Bucks can be heard grunting a challenge to another buck.

Another sound that can alert you to the presence of a buck is the sound it makes while thrashing a sapling before and during the breeding season. Of course, bucks fight for breeding rights, and the sounds of their battles can be heard over long distances as they struggle to get their legs braced and push and grind antlers together.

Deer will also "blow" when they are startled by a scent they fear. Often, when a deer begins to blow, flight is next. But they are sometimes curious and will circle to get downwind or get a better look to confirm the smell. But don't bet on a big buck doing this.

SMELL

Wind can be your ally or your biggest enemy. Your scent is frightening to most deer. Because they don't understand it, the scent signals danger. Smell is the one sense that they never question. The better you understand how deer react to "dangerous" odors, the better you will be able to exploit a deer's sense of smell.

If the wind is steady from one direction, hunt into it. A steady wind is the friend of the still-hunter. (I carry and use a product called *Smoke-In-A-Bottle*. It is a white powder in a squeeze bottle. Squirted in the air, it allows the hunter to read wind direction. I rely on it, checking the wind constantly to make sure that the deer I am hunting won't catch my scent.)

Don't ever fool yourself into believing that a deer might not smell you. If the wind is at your back the deer know you're there and you have a limited chance of success.

When you scout or hunt, watch where you walk and what you brush up against. Your scent will transfer to the brush, leaving a faint, lingering smell that warns animals of your presence long after you are gone. One habit that many hunters have is to pull a twig off with their fingers, idly play with it while they walk and eventually discard it. If you indulge in this, you're advertising your presence.

Scent control is just as important to the tree stand hunter. When you choose your stand location, pick a spot that takes advantage of the prevailing wind, and pick an alternate for those days when the wind is coming from the other direction.

If the wind appears to be swirling, it's better to back out of the hunt area and try another tactic than to risk blowing a well-scouted location by spooking the animals.

There are times when you can use your scent to advantage. If you have good visibility, your scent can act as a driver, pushing deer out ahead of you. This tactic has saved the day for many hunters over the years.

Perry Parmelee with a huge mule deer buck he tagged on a hunt in southeast Idaho. Photo courtesy Perry Parmelee.

Fred Rountry of Spokane, Washington on a December hunt for Sitka blacktails on Kodiak Island. Gary Lewis photo.

Chapter 7

THE HUNT

STILL-HUNTING

I remember, Mrs. Parrish, my kindergarten teacher at Kalama Elementary School, explaining that prey species have eyes that are set on the sides of their face, allowing them to catch the movement of approaching predators whether winged, four-footed, or two-footed.

She said humans are like the wolf, the bear, and the lion. Our eyes are in the front of our face, allowing us to focus on our prey.

Technology has turned man, the ultimate predator, into man, the consumer. We consume power, petroleum, potato chips, polyester, and prescriptions. We run around in circles, from home to school to job to grocery store and home again in the relentless pursuit of more goods to consume. Every year we get better at it, whirling faster and faster in our circles.

It's easy to bring our lifestyle to the woods and deserts, but it's not welcome there. In fact, it is counter-productive if the goal is to tie a tag on a deer. To succeed, we must become predators again.

Still-hunters do well to emulate the cat. Watch how a farm cat hunts. It may sit patiently, watching and listening, or it may walk slowly, picking its way along, alert and ready. Its movements are deliberate, with little wasted motion, watchful. Its movements are swift only when it is pouncing on a field mouse, or when danger threatens.

Leave behind the fast-paced world of the consumer and become the cat. Hunt with the wind in your face to keep your scent from reaching your prey.

Have you ever noticed how a deer can stand rooted in one place for ten minutes or longer, while he processes information brought to him on the wind? Practice standing still for ten minutes the next time you walk in deer habitat.

Move as slow as a feeding deer. Take a step. Pause and look around, moving your eyes first. Watch for movement. Test the air with your nose. Sometimes you can smell the animal before you see him.

Wait thirty seconds or a minute or two minutes. Then take another step and scan the woods from this new vantage. You are seeing a new view of the world framed in a different series of trees, looking for the horizontal line of a deer's back or the crook of a leg against the vertical world of trees and brush.

No other animal sounds like a human in the woods. *Step, step, step, step, step.* Deer don't sound like that, squirrels don't sound like that. Coyotes don't sound like that. Only humans do. Don't let the cadence of your footsteps give you away.

Move slower than you ever imagined you could. Expect to see a deer. In good habitat, you will. If you move carefully and cautiously, you *will* see them before they see you.

When still-hunting, never take more than two steps at a time. Any step you take without first thoroughly scanning the terrain, is a give-away move to the deer.

As long as the deer don't smell you first, they are counting on their hearing and vision to protect them. Deer instantly spot movement. This ability to spot quick movement is what keeps them alive. Motionless, you can watch deer unobserved. Make a quick movement and you send the alarm that a predator is near.

Take light steps to test the ground before you put your weight down. Glance at the patch of trail ahead and subconsciously chart your path. Let the sole of your foot feel for a stick that might snap, or gravel that might grind, or dry leaves that might crunch. Still-hunters should wear shoes or boots with a light sole that allow the hunter to detect noisemakers before they alert game.

Go slow. Ask yourself, *Why am I in such a hurry to spook these animals?*

Move from cover to cover. If you have to cross a wide-open clearing or a bench devoid of cover, find a way around it, even if it means a wide detour. Your target animal might not see you cross the opening, but other animals will. The presence of a predator will make non-target animals more wary and their attitudes will be picked up by the deer. You can't afford to let this happen. You may have done everything else right. Don't take the easy, wide-open route if it will blow everything you have worked for up to that point.

Spend extra time watching from the shade of a boulder or a tree. Keep your face and binoculars in the shade.

Binoculars are the second most important tool the still-hunter carries. Don't leave them in the truck. Don't leave them in your pack. They do the most good when you are using them. If you are still-hunting you will use them often.

Binoculars are not just for long-distance viewing. Through my binoculars, I have seen game at fifteen yards in heavy cover that I wouldn't have been able to confirm had I not had swift access to my glasses. I used to leave the binoculars in my pack

Steve Lakey took his mule deer buck on the last day of deer season. Photo by Chris Lakey.

because of the thin strap that dug into the back of my neck. Finally, I did something about it and bought a comfortable neckstrap and a restraint system that holds the glasses against my chest while not in use. My binoculars have become so important that I feel severely handicapped if I forget them.

Still-hunting is a solo sport. It's hard enough for one person to do well. If still-hunting appeals to you, don't handicap yourself by bringing a partner. However, two still-hunters can hunt a strip of timber separately, working into the wind. If one hunter bumps a deer, it may sneak toward his quieter partner.

Successful still-hunting is as much about attitude as it is about stealth. Tell yourself that you will see the deer before they see you. Convince yourself. Believe that the slower you move, the more deer you will see.

WAITING

We are not accustomed to waiting, to spending long minutes without moving. Our fast-paced lives have programmed us for action. We want to move, to see, to do. But think about it, if you were at home, you could sit in one place for thirty minutes reading a book. Learn to be at home in your hunting area, reading the wind, the smells, the sign, the shapes of trees, and shrubs.

A deer can outwait most hunters because he is already home, he is not in a hurry to get anywhere—unless he sees you moving.

ONCE, ON AN EVENING blacktail hunt, I picked my way up an old logging road and moved to the edge of an opening in the trees. I stopped for a few minutes to watch. Soon, I heard a hoof strike the ground. I waited. There was no more sound. But I *had* heard something.

I started forward and saw the horizontal line of a deer's back through a screen of shrubbery. He was looking at me. When he turned his head to look for an escape route, I saw antlers. He was a spike buck who, to be legal, had to have at least one forked antler. I watched him go.

He was a young buck, and I educated him. In turn, older bucks have educated me.

Once, I was hunting in a sub-alpine forest and approached a small cluster of bushes and boulders in the midst of a stand of adult fir trees.

I heard that same unmistakable sound of a hoof striking the ground as a deer rose out of its bed. Close. I stopped and waited and listened. There was no more sound. After a few minutes passed, I asked myself if I had imagined it. *Maybe,* I thought, *I heard a branch fall to the earth.* I began to think about my next move. I would detour around the brush pile and work to the edge of the timber and work my way down along the creek bed…

After another five minutes of waiting, my thoughts turned into action and I moved forward. The deer had out-waited and outwitted me. As soon as I moved to the left, he circled to the right. I could hear his heavy hooves striking the hard ground as he bounced away, keeping the boulders and the bushes between us. I never even saw what he looked like. 🦌

RUNNING

Almost all our experiences in deer country teach us that going slow is better than going fast. When we move too fast we spook the deer. We train our reactions to be slow, and deliberate. But that can also make us tentative. There are times when you have to push, be aggressive. Let your experience override your instinct. Sometimes you have to flat out run to cover a lot of ground in a hurry to catch a glimpse of a buck trying to make it out the back door, while you watch the front.

A two-man drive put Gary Lewis into position to anchor this nice 4-point mule deer.

ONCE, MY FRIEND JAMES Flaherty missed a shot at a running buck. The deer bounded away through the sage and junipers. I stood there watching, and wished I'd been in position for the shot. Instead of standing there wishing he'd timed the shot better, James took off at a dead run. Suddenly I was alone.

James pushed that deer to the edge of a cliff and then followed it along the edge, waiting for another opportunity. When I finally caught up with him, the opportunity was mine. I shot the buck. But I never would have had the chance at it if James had followed my instinct "to watch" instead of his desire and experience.

HUNTING FROM A TREE STAND

Hunting deer from up above isn't just for East Coast whitetail-hunters anymore. Blacktails, western whitetails, and some mule deer are creatures of habit too. The careful hunter with an insight into the habits of the animals and the terrain can put the tree stand to effective use.

The tree stand allows a hunter to remain undetected by most deer under most conditions. In fact, year after year, hunting from above is the way that the most successful blacktail trophy hunters take their animals.

A public-land blacktail buck who has lived through several hunting seasons is one of the hardest trophies to take. Staying undetected in his living room is the most important skill a hunter can learn. A carefully placed stand can be the key to your success.

Use a stand that is comfortable, safe, and quiet. Place it high enough so that you are above a deer's line-of-sight and downstream of the prevailing wind. Wear a safety harness. Falling from a perch twenty feet up a tree is a terrible way to wake up from a nap.

Wear soft, camouflaged clothing, including gloves and face mask—except during rifle season. Rifle hunters should wear some hunter orange.

This climbing tree stand, owned by Brian Smith, helped put the author twenty-five feet up a loblolly pine and in position to take two whitetails on successive days in South Carolina. Gary Lewis photo.

Choose a tree with enough foliage that the branches will obscure your silhouette. When traveling to and from your stand, wear rubber boots to keep your scent from warning animals.

Use the same path coming and going to your stand. Don't touch vegetation. Following these guidelines will keep you from spreading human scent. For the same reason, and to allow you to stay stationary on a stand, carry a plastic urine bottle and use it while in the tree. Carry your waste out with you and dump it far from your stand.

Scouting is the key to successful stand placement. Start with topo maps of your hunt area and narrow down your options to a few choice locations. Then go scouting. Visit each of your choices and target feeding areas. Brushy benches, springs, small meadows, and slide areas provide browse and forbs that high country deer rely on for the feed to carry them through the fall. Recent logging operations, burns, pastures, and farm land are also good bets at lower elevations.

Finding bedding areas is a little more of a challenge, but it is the key to your success. Employ binoculars to watch deer from afar. Glass feeding areas and watch deer in early morning as they head toward their beds. Be there in the evening to watch them come down the trails.

Bucks will often bed in areas of heavy vegetation or timber within a quarter-mile of their principal feeding area. Look for benches that offer a view of terrain above and below. Look for patches of manzanita or other vegetation that will allow a buck to hear the approach of a predator. Pay special attention to the edges of timber islands on high slopes or points where a deer can lay with his back to a tree and watch the approaches.

Determine the travel routes between bedding and feeding grounds and find the terrain features that funnel deer. These are the core areas that deer use day after day. After locating the travel corridor, hang your stand. This is best done during the middle of the day when deer are bedded. Check the prevailing wind and hang your stand on the downwind side of the trail. When you return to hunt, be in place well before first light.

Most mule deer are more difficult to pattern than whitetails and blacktails. But some mule deer are vulnerable when they are feeding consistently on agricultural lands. Watch from far away and you'll see where they go in the morning and where they come from in the evening. Learn their patterns and you can hunt these mule deer from a stand in the morning and evening and by spot-and-stalk during the day.

Mule deer are also vulnerable when traveling to and from water. If terrain features funnel deer, you can position a stand for an ambush. Look for saddles used by deer crossing between canyons or any natural barrier such as a rock pile or fallen timber.

The basic types of tree stands are: *climbing stands* that utilize a tree with a limbless trunk; *hang-on stands* that are light but require screw-in or strap-on steps; and *heavy ladder stands*. Always use a safety rope or harness when hunting from a tree stand.

Choose a tree with a diameter at least as large as your waist. Trees this size are safe to climb and offer better concealment.

How far away from the trail? Bowhunters should set up between 15 and 25 yards away, while gun hunters have the luxury of moving back a little: 50 to 75 yards from where they expect to see deer.

Put your tree stand high in the tree but be mindful of the shot angle that you will be forced to make. At least 15 feet above the ground will put you over the approaching deer's line of sight. If the wind is prone to swirling in the area you have chosen for a stand, it would be better to raise the stand even higher, to 20, 30, or even 35 feet above the ground.

ON A HUNT FOR WHITETAILS one year, I put my stand 18 feet up in a tree. The wind was gusting and changing directions. I wished I'd put the stand up higher, but it was too late. With only a half-hour of light left, I couldn't afford to be moving around and making noise. I could hear a deer approaching in the dry leaves. She never looked up, but she caught some hint of scent. She bolted suddenly and changed directions.

The next day, I hunted in a section that had been logged within the last two years. A number of tall pines remained. I went 30 feet up into one of them. I shot a doe and waited to see if a buck would come out. One did. I could hear him coming through the short pine and brush to my left. I saw antlers and then his head and neck emerged. The first thing he did before he moved into the open was to check the wind for scent. I was high above him but he smelled something. As I swung the rifle to my shoulder, he spun and retreated into the brush. 🦌

If you will be hunting with a bow, place your stand on the trail side of the tree for the best shooting clearance. If you hunt with a rifle, you can set your stand on the opposite side of the trunk to better conceal yourself. (This also allows you to use the tree as a rest.)

Keep comfort in mind. The more comfortable you make your perch, the longer you will stay. A padded seat is nice and so is a footrest. If you place your stand where a thick limb can double as a rest, giving you something to lean against, so much the better. Again, wear a safety harness. Too many hunters have died from falling asleep and falling from a comfortable tree stand.

After your stand is in place, trim limbs that might affect your shot in all possible shooting lanes. Pocket-pruning shears are the best tool for this.

STALKING

The most exciting part of the hunt is the time between when you spot your quarry and

Travis Fields with a buck he took during Oregon's archery season. Pre-season scouting helped him pattern deer movement and allowed him to be in place for the shot. Photo courtesy Travis Fields.

when you squeeze the trigger or release your arrow. The spotting and stalking window in time might take the better part of a day.

The careful hunter will often spot his game before the game sees him. It might be a blacktail buck in his afternoon bed or a feeding mule deer browsing along a rocky ledge just after daybreak.

Often, the hunter needs to sneak within range—within 50 yards with a bow, and under 200 yards with a rifle. Depending upon circumstances such as terrain, proximity of other animals, and wind direction, the stalk might take minutes or last for hours.

I WAS HUNTING BACK to camp one warm September afternoon when I spotted a deer standing in the shade of a pine tree. Its head was down in a bush and all I could see were its flanks and hindquarters. Nocking an arrow, I took stock of the situation.

I was eighty yards away. The ground was covered with pumice rock, making every step noisy. I was wearing a light boot that fit more like a tennis shoe, so I could be fairly quiet when I needed to be.

As I watched, the deer scraped out a bed and laid down. I still couldn't see whether it was a buck or a doe. Now just the top of its back was showing. I waited a few minutes. The wind was still in my favor, blowing to the right. I started across the pumice field.

I kept a tree between us and moved closer, each step a struggle to keep quiet. I heard the pumice grind beneath my foot and I stopped, frozen, watching the deer's body. It had stiffened at the sound of my step.

A few minutes passed and the deer relaxed. I was within forty yards now. With the animal lying down I still had no shot at the vitals so I waited some more. When I closed in to thirty, I could see that the deer was a doe, legal to take in the area I was hunting. She was looking away from me but she was alert and listening. *How close could I get?*

Suddenly standing up, she walked stiff-legged into the sun and looked back at me. I drew my bow to full draw and she presented a broadside shot. I had a moment's decision to shoot or pass. The deer walked. What a thrill. 🌿

Other stalks will take longer and may require more planning and strategy to execute. Wind direction will probably be your first concern. You will want to stalk a bedded buck with the wind in your face. In the mountains, the wind can change as valley air temperatures rise in the morning or fall in the late afternoon. Take suspected wind changes into account before beginning a long stalk on a bedded buck.

Take time to study the approach to your target. One thing you can count on is that terrain features will look different up close. Memorize where the buck is bedded by triangulation with prominent trees, snags, boulders or land contours.

Better than memorization is mapping. Pack a small notebook and a pencil. Decide in advance where you will stand or rest to take your shot. Then map the route you will take to get there, moving from landmark to landmark.

If you hunt with a partner, determine a set of hand signals in advance and resist the urge to take a look at the buck while you move in. Instead, look at your partner for direction. He or she will tell you if the buck is getting nervous or starting to move.

That blacktail you spotted in some patch of alder and second-growth fir, or that muley on a boulder-strewn ridge, has three senses that protect him from predators, whether cougar, bobcat, coyote, black bear, or human. You must defeat his vision by using whatever cover is available. You must defeat his hearing by moving silently. You must defeat his sense of smell by using the wind to your advantage.

Deer, elk, and antelope rely on their incredible peripheral vision to keep them safe. They constantly turn their heads as they browse, frequently looking up, around, and behind.

Think about what alerts *you* to the presence of game or other hunters as you walk through the forest. It's movement. Maybe you catch the first glimpse from the corner of your eye. You turn your head to look and then maybe you see the grayish coat of an autumn mule deer or distinguish the red and black plaid of a hunting shirt.

Similarly, your movement is most often what spooks a deer. Once it's seen you moving, it stops to look to see what you are, to determine whether or not you are a threat. If you move while he is looking, then all you'll see of him is the white of his rump as he disappears among the trees.

As with anything, practice will make you better. Even before I started hunting for big game I practiced getting close to animals without them knowing I was there. I stalked house cats, squirrels, rabbits, and deer for fun, learning a little in the process.

Once, on a hilltop outside of the Eastern Oregon town of Paulina, I stalked a herd of deer in the fog. There was little wind and clouds lay like a blanket on the hill. Spooking the deer once, I waited until the herd vanished in the mist, gave them a few minutes to settle down, then closed in again.

The fog kept them from seeing my approach. The wind blew from them to me. The frosty grass silenced the sound of my approach.

I had a good broadside look at a standing deer. One shot ended that hunt in the first hour of the season.

HUNTING BEDDING AREAS ALONG RIDGES AND ROLLING HILLS

If you find yourself hunting a long ridgeline during the time of day when deer are likely to be bedded, you can use a simple strategy adapted from still-hunting.

Travel parallel to the ridge, keeping your head below the ridgeline. Move slowly against the wind. About every 75 yards hook to the crest and peer over, looking into likely bedding spots with your binoculars. Bucks often bed up against rocky outcroppings or under isolated trees.

If a patch of brush is thick enough to conceal a bedded deer, discreetly toss a stone into the cover and wait to see if a deer stands up or bolts out.

This 'hooking' technique can earn you a shot at an unsuspecting buck.

TECHNIQUES FOR HUNTING ON WINDY DAYS

Once I hunted with my wife, Merrilee, and our friends James and Denise Flaherty, for antlerless mule deer on a ranch. We watched deer in the evening and saw them bedded in the fields at night. Later, the wind began to howl and the windows in the bunkhouse soon rattled in their panes. The storm raged all night and all the next day.

In the morning, the deer quit the fields early and headed for shelter from the wind. We saw three deer feeding in the corner of a field and watched them head for the high ridge before we could plan a stalk. Three more does crossed the field and the road onto an adjoining piece of property.

Denise spotted a herd of twenty deer coming down off a ridge. We watched them cross a road and skyline on another ridge, running into the wind. We followed.

It was a half-hour later, not yet eight in the morning, when we jumped a small buck and watched him work away from us on the hillside. On top, the wind blew with such force that breathing was difficult. The deer had escaped.

James and I skipped lunch and went out again, setting our faces in the wind to hunt bedding areas.

A long hogback runs east to west and slopes off to each side. We hunted the north slope, spread 60 yards apart. We looked into draws, washouts, and below the rimrock.

James bumped a buck from a little hollow where it had lain protected from the wind. It was a bowl, about forty yards in diameter and about eight feet deep. The deer had bedded beneath sagebrush in the center of the bowl. We watched a tall forked horn buck bounce away and then stop to look back.

It was afternoon when we found six does bedded in the bottom of a high, freshly-plowed valley where they had 400 yards of visibility in all directions and protection from the high wind.

We crawled on our hands and knees to peer down at them, then settled in to take our shots. I lined my crosshair on a big-bodied deer that was bedded apart from the group and missed. 🍃

Mule deer like a strong wind about as much as we do. When the wind blows hard, they head for sheltered canyons, draws, hollows, and benches where they bed on the downwind side of terrain features that will protect them from the harsh wind.

When the wind blows hard, hunt protected cover areas to increase your chances of finding the animals.

TWO-MAN DRIVES

A two-man drive can help you to roust a bedded buck from his bed. Here's how it works:

Two hunters work through bedding cover, parallel to each other, usually within eyesight of each other. The deer focus on danger coming from one hunter and sneak into the path of the other. I have used this technique in three feet of snow on Kodiak Island *and* in the desert. Variations can be applied almost anywhere deer are hunted.

Bucks may bed on high hogbacks where they can make their escape down either side or through the trees.

ONCE WE FOUND THREE does and a buck bedded where they could watch a three-hundred-yard rocky expanse. Nothing could approach from that direction without one of those deer spotting it. A strong breeze blew the wind from the junipers at their back. Nothing could approach from behind them without them smelling it first. In this case they *smelled* us.

The third day of the season was the warmest yet. We hiked onto the mountain where I had taken a good buck during the previous season; but water was scarce and fresh deer tracks were more scarce. There were more tracks down lower, close to water and ranchlands. Still, we looked into draws and scanned beneath the rim for holed-up mule deer. A big buck was our goal and we didn't expect to find him in the lowlands.

At one point, we heard coyotes close by, running down a deer, unseen for the thick juniper trees on the ridge.

As morning gave way to afternoon, we changed tactics and hunted the bedding areas on the slopes of the mountain. Nothing. We hunted downhill and looked over the edge of the canyon into likely bedding spots. Nothing.

There is a point in a hunt when intensity lets off like a pressure-relief valve. We hit that spot at about 1:30 in the afternoon. Even as we let our guard down and began to joke and whisper, we kept watch. At other times like that, we've come upon deer in their beds and blown our opportunity when our guard was down.

We would have walked right by those deer if it hadn't been for that cagey old buck getting nervous. He hooked a doe in the backside and she leaped away.

I saw gray flash through the junipers and pulled up my binoculars. A doe. Then a second and third, made their escape. James had his rifle up, ready. No antlers.

Still we watched, waiting. There! The buck headed in the opposite direction the does had taken. James swung his rifle to his shoulder as the deer bounded away. He fired and missed and the deer vanished into the junipers, leaving me with no shot. We followed.

As we had done for three days, we went into two-man-drive mode, walking forty yards apart, parallel to each other through the junipers along the rim.

The sun beat down and there was little shade. We followed the buck as he made his way up and down through washes and around rocky out-croppings. Catching glimpses of gray-brown hair and golden antler through the green junipers and silver sage, we kept following..

The buck turned a hard left and came running out into the sunlight. I threw my rifle to my shoulder, swinging the crosshairs across his body. Leading him in the brief opening in the trees, I snicked off the safety and squeezed the trigger.

The 160-grain Nosler Partition threw that buck for a loop, slamming him to the ground.

After the shot I was shaking. I could tell, even from far away, that I had killed a big buck. Pacing off the distance allowed me to calm my nerves. I counted 137 yards. Then came the slaps on the back for a great end to a hard hunt. We admired the antlers and the fine shiny coat and breathed in the familiar scent of a "buck of the sage."

The deer was heavy. His antlers taped 28-1/2 inches wide, with four points per side, and hooked eye guards.

It took two hours to cape, skin, and quarter, then another two hours to pack it a mile and a half out to the road.

We found a spring burbling water into a cattle tank. That was why the deer weren't bedded up as high as they usually are at that time of year. With little rain, other sources had dried up. My buck had bedded in the forest rather than on the mountain to be closer to water. (Something to keep in mind.) And I won't forget how a two-man drive allowed one hunter to push a big buck to another hunter who worked parallel!

We cupped hands to catch the water, letting it run down, cool and refreshing over our heads as the moon came up over the mountain. 🌿

HUNT THE "EDGE" HABITAT

I CROSSED THE ROAD from camp into the timber, grateful for the cover the trees afforded me from the driving rain. It had been falling since 4:00 A.M. and the treetops were saturated, leaving precious few places where one could find dry shelter. Waiting for first light, I was grateful for the pound of the rain and the howl of the wind. The rain would mask the sounds I made walking. The wind would blow in a constant direction. I wished they'd stop for my own comfort, but knew they wouldn't.

A dull glow filled the somber sky and filtered through the trees. I began to move.

Slipping from tree to tree, I paused to peer ahead through the rain and watched for the gleam of eye or antler, the flicker of ears. The hill leveled out in front of me and, watching from under a large fir tree, I spotted movement. I saw their ears first and the horizontal line of mouse-gray backs above the manzanita. They had seen me too and moved away, stiff-legged and watchful. I put the binoculars to my eyes and could make out no antlers. So I watched them go, one by one, fading into the trees and the fog.

Angling off the plateau, I aimed for the shelf below and the creek canyon. There were other hunters in the woods. They would see the deer I had moved. Hopefully, I would see a deer they pushed in front of me.

I moved through a stand of jack pines, where in another year I'd jumped a deer from its bed. I eased through and watched the shelf below me. The forest floor was carpeted with the fallen needles from pines and white fir that towered above. Protected from the high winds, there was little blowdown. Without much sunlight making it through the old-growth timber the underbrush was sparse. Standing on the sidehill beneath the arms of a tall pine, I watched the line of trees to my left.

He stepped out of the timber, moving off the hill. Stopping to look for danger at the edge of a tiny meadow, he spotted me at the same time I saw him, the shine of his antlers plain from seventy-five yards away. I snugged the gun up against my shoulder and put the stock against my cheek, letting the sights drift across his body to stop behind the muscle and bone of his foreleg. Slipping the safety switch to fire, I squeezed the trigger, feeling the push of the rifle against my shoulder, the report drifting away up the mountain.

I followed his tracks for seventy yards to the place he had come to rest. He lay beside a rotten log on a bed of pine needles. The rain pounded down and soaked me to the skin. But I was oblivious; my hunt was over. 🍂

If you're hunting in early October, the rut doesn't begin for another month. Barring a heavy snow, the deer will still mainly be on their summer

Kreg Roth (right) took this nice mule deer buck while hunting with guide, Skip Geer and High Lonesome Hunts.

range. Bucks will be found alone or to-gether in groups of two or three.

Bucks tend to leave the bottom-land and best browse areas to the females. If the deer you are seeing are does and fawns, move to higher, drier ground to look for bucks. Hunt "the edge" areas where ridgetops give way to timber and trees give way to meadows or agricultural lands.

Note the contour of the land and the natural lanes of travel. Dry creek beds, grown-over logging roads, and canyons are good places to start. A good buck won't use an escape-route that will leave him exposed.

As yourself what the obstacles are. Trails must detour around rock out-croppings, so well-used trails will be obvious. The animals will move around on opening day. If you're posted along one of these routes, chances are higher that you will see animals.

Don't quit at midday. Carry your lunch and water with you. A buck will be laying down somewhere. He'll have a spot from which he can see in many directions or a spot in the thick stuff where anybody approaching will alert him with their noise. If it's warm, the buck will bed in the shade and always have an escape route.

Watch the movement of other hunters. I've often seen animals spooked by hunters who were oblivious to the fact that they were pushing game.

If fortune smiles and the deer we see have antlers, we'll pack our winter's meat back down. If the deer are quick and our reactions slow, we'll have the memory of the sun coming up and going down on a good day afield.

TRAILING WOUNDED GAME

MY DISTANCE ESTIMATION was right, my form was good and the release was smooth, but the deer stepped forward as the arrow left the string. The shaft buried into its hip and the deer hunched up and lunged ahead, tail corkscrewing, legs churning through the underbrush. I stood still.

My emotions were mixed. It was the second week of the season. I had hunted hard before I took that shot, but the hunt was about to get a lot harder. I intended to make a quick, clean kill, but things didn't turn out that way.

I was hunting the Sisters Wilderness Area on the edge of a lake in Central Oregon with my good friends Dave and Jon Hamilton. The weather had been dry as it usually is during the early bow season. I had seen plenty of deer, but because of the crackling groundcover, had trouble getting close enough for a shot.

We woke that Sunday morning to find that a gentle rain had fallen and it looked like more was coming. Eating a hurried breakfast, we anticipated quieter hunting. Just after 6:15 we split up. Dave head South toward the rim and I headed West. Jon slept in, planning to fish the lake later in the morning.

I saw the deer browsing on a side-hill parallel to the trail I was on. I waited until its head was behind a tree and settled my thirty-yard pin on the vitals. The arrow struck a twig in its path and careened wildly away. The animal trotted forward nervously and looked back. I shot again, this time placing the forty-yard pin just behind the shoulder. The deer stepped forward at the sound of the shot and the arrow buried deep into its hip. There is an artery in the hip that I hoped I had hit. The crashing ended as the deer burst out of the brush and headed for the rim. I looked at my watch. It was 6:30 A.M.

I waited about five minutes then removed my fluorescent orange flagging from my fanny pack and marked the spot I had shot from. I visually located the spot where the deer had stood and memorized it. I then turned around and headed back to camp. I was elated that I had connected and full of nervous energy.

Back at camp, I roused Jon and told him about the job we had ahead of us. We cooked breakfast and sat down to wait. We decided to wait five hours and then pick up the trail, hoping the wound would force the animal to lie down and bleed out.

Dave came in about 8:00 and reported that he'd seen a wounded deer below the rim. Having seen no other hunters in the area, we surmised it must be the one we were after. At 10:00 it started to sprinkle and we knew that we needed to get on the trail before the rain washed away the sign.

We found my arrow in the trail and marked its location with orange flagging. The arrow shaft was bloody and had tissue and hair in the broadhead. One blade was missing. Immediately we found more bloody tissue and also marked that spot.

We felt confident by this time. Based upon the color of the blood and the look of the tissue, I guessed the arrow had angled up into the kidney and that we would soon find the expired deer. But it wasn't to be. Soon the drops of blood became harder to find. We had to look at our back trail, marked with orange flagging, to get a general indication of the animal's path. When we couldn't find any sign we worked in ever-widening circles until we picked it up again.

Jon had brought along binoculars and periodically scanned the sides of the bowl we were in. At times we got discouraged with the tedium and one or the other would attempt to bolster spirits. I passed out beef jerky and we each carried water. The rain had let up and then resumed in earnest at about the same time we lost the trail. It was noon.

We sat under the rim at the edge of a clearing and watched, thinking our own private thoughts about the whole enterprise. I don't know what the others were doing, but I was praying. The rain was washing away the sign.

Across the bowl, we heard a loud crack. A deer had stood up and broken a branch. Jon put the binoculars on it but the wound would have been on the far side of the animal. We couldn't tell if it was the right deer or not. There was nothing else to do but go after it.

Dave followed the deer and I went to where it had bedded. I found no blood. However the deer seemed to be dragging a leg.

We followed its tracks then, finding no blood in its unhurried gait. We trailed it into a lush area along the banks of a creek and then I found blood again. We were close, but didn't know which way it was headed. I passed around more jerky. Then Jon saw it. The deer had doubled back and was walking uphill again. I don't know what I would have done without the help of those two extra pairs of eyes.

We were close now and we pushed. Finding blood more frequently, our confidence grew again. As we moved toward the rim, tracking became easier. Instead of going into cover, the deer moved in a straight line across an open plain. The dragging leg was more pronounced and we were able to follow the tracks at a run.

When we lost the track we were able to find it again by looking at it from another angle, seeing the shadow inside the print.

Finding no refuge uphill, the animal switched directions and went down. We ran again, catching glimpses now and then, pausing only briefly to confirm the track. Being familiar with the area, we were able to anticipate the direction of travel.

The deer paused to lay down in some trees near a well-used hiking trail close to the lake. It presented me with an easy shot. I had drawn my bow to shoot when I heard voices. I couldn't shoot when there might be somebody behind my deer. The deer got up and walked down to the edge of the lake. Then it laid down again in some driftwood at the water's edge. I was above the animal and took the shot at fifty yards. The arrow went high. And the deer went into the lake. I couldn't believe it.

A rubber raft isn't something I normally pack along on a bowhunt. The deer swam 150 yards out, not even pausing to look back. There were fishermen out there but they didn't seem to notice. I could only think of one thing to do.

I ran along the edge of the lake until I came to a fellow taking a break from fishing. Imagine me, camouflage head to toe, face paint and out of breath from running, with a bow in my hand.

"Excuse me, sir...."

Though he wasn't a hunter, Jake was a fisherman, and after all, there isn't much difference. He could see the fix I was in and consented to take me out there.

He had a twelve-foot rubber raft and an electric motor. It was the perfect set-up—nice and quiet. We eased up alongside the deer and I ended it with an arrow to the spine. We tied it off and pulled the deer to shore. 🌿

I learned a good deal about trailing wounded animals from this experience. Patience is paramount. By waiting for the deer to calm down, we were given the added advantage that the wound was causing the animal to stiffen and slow down.

Persistence was also key. Had we given up when we lost the track and just rationalized that maybe the deer was going to be okay, there would have been no meat in the freezer and the coyotes and ravens would have gotten an easy meal.

You have to also know when to push and when to wait. We felt that we had to push our deer because the bleeding stopped when it wasn't moving.

If you can find it, check

TRACKING WOUNDED GAME

- Hunt with friends who partner in all aspects of the hunt. Choose responsible companions who share in the duties of recovery.
- Examine the clues provided at the point of impact.
- Use surveyor's flagging to mark the trail, to help show direction of travel, as well as to help you find your way back.
- Measure the stride of the animal to enable you to find the next tracks when you temporarily lose the trail.
- Keep an eye on the trail ahead. You may be pushing the deer while you are tracking it.
- When the trail goes dry, don't give up. Circle your last sign in ever increasing circles, until you find another clue.

the arrow for blood, bone, tissue, and hair. These give clues to where the animal was hit and how long you must wait before tracking.

Frothy blood and tissue might indicate a lung-shot animal. Clumps of white hair at point of impact might indicate a shot in the belly or legs. Dark red blood could indicate a shot to the kidney.

A heart-shot can be followed in ten or twenty minutes. A lung-shot deer should be given an hour or more to expire. Give a gut shot deer eight hours, more or less.

Every situation is different. We started trailing earlier than we planned due to the rain.

Always use flagging when trailing an injured animal. When you lose the blood trail you can often find it again by looking back and discerning the animal's general direction. Often the only sign you find will be a speck of blood on a pine needle or a smear on a leaf that the deer brushed up against as it walked by. Get on your hands and knees to look for sign along the animal's path.

Sometimes you'll find blood but won't be able to determine the direction of travel. Find a fallen log and look at where the blood splashed out from the animal's exertion. The direction of travel will be on the opposite side of the log from where you found the blood.

Use binoculars, or have your partner use them. Your quarry will be checking its backtrail frequently. Keep your voices low, and remember the hunt is not over.

Most of all, keep after it. The game deserves your dedication and the sport needs good hunters.

GEAR

When our youngest daughter was two-years-old and saw a deer or a picture of one, she would exclaim, "Ah, bucka. See bucka!"

We would tell her, "Right. Deer," or, "Buck deer."

"Yah. Gear," she'd say.

I think she had a point. Every hunter needs to consider the gear they will take into the field.

During archery season I wear camouflage from head to toe. When your weapon is a bent stick and a pointed shaft, you need every edge you can get. When hunting with a shotgun or a rifle among other hunters I make concessions to safety, opting for some hunter orange in my outfit.

Hands and face should be camouflaged when archery hunting. I use mosquito-net camouflage gloves to kill the reflection from my hands when I hunt with a bow. And I put grease paint on my face to help my skin blend with the foliage. Sometimes it helps to put leafy twigs in your hatband as well, to break up the outline of your head and shoulders as you approach your prey.

Smell may be the deer and elk's most relied-upon sense. They may take time to stop and look when they see you coming, but when the wind blows your scent to them they don't think twice. They run for the deepest cover they can find.

Plan your stalk with the wind in mind. Some bowhunters hang a downy feather or a thread from their bow. Once I stayed with a herd of elk for over two hours as I monitored the feather hanging from my bow. When the wind shifted I would back off or change my direction until I was downwind again.

Cover scent can help to some degree. But cover scent doesn't *kill* your body's natural scent, it just mingles with it. Wearing cover scents or not, when you close to within 50 yards of a wary game animal you need to be downwind or the game will be quickly over—leaving you the loser.

As with defeating a deer's vision, to get close without him hearing your approach, you must slow down. Every step is a potential alarm going off in the animal's brain telling it to flee the country.

Good boots are essential but can be noisy on fallen branches and dried leaves. There are several ways to deaden the sound of your footfalls.

When you must get close, take your shoes off. When all that is between you and the rocks are a thin pair of socks, you don't move fast. Each step is taken with extreme care. Every potential snapping stick is felt with your toes or the ball of your foot before you put your weight down. I have hunted in moccasins and three layers of wool socks. The stealth you can achieve with just a strip of leather or wool between you and the earth is astounding. The soft leather or woven wool absorbs the sounds of pumice grating or the snap of twigs.

Moccasins can be tied to a belt or packframe. When a stalk must be made, the hunter simply shucks the boots and slips on the moccasins.

A third way to add stealth to your stalk is with a polyester fleece over-boot. A product called Baer's Feet slips on over the boot. The sound of dry leaves crackling or twigs breaking underfoot are muffled by the heavy one-inch pile material on the sole. What makes these ideal for later-season hunters is the fact that moisture and cold won't penetrate to the feet through the fleece and boots as it will through moccasins or socks alone.

Baer's Feet won't add weight to your load and can be tied out of the way on your pack, ready to be used as needed. You can find them through archery dealers or *Cabela's*.

Still-hunters who spend a lot of time in heavy cover should consider other elements of their gear as well. Nylon caps, backpacks, and fanny packs are noisy in thick brush. Fleece, chamois, or saddlecloth are good, quiet alternatives.

And of course, sound is only one of the elements to consider. Remember to keep the wind in your face to get closer to game. *Smoke in a Bottle* can help you dope the wind. Simply pop the top with your thumbnail and squeeze. The white powder puffs ride the air currents, giving a visible indicator of what the wind is doing.

Of course, gear is never a substitute for good hunting skill but the right gear can go a long way toward helping you bag your buck.

Travis Fields with his record-book mule deer. This buck scored 180-2/8 Pope and Young. Scouting and focus are the keys to Travis' bowhunting success. Photo courtesy Travis Fields.

Gary Lewis on Prince of Wales Island. Photo by Don Lewis.

Chapter 8

NORTH TO ALASKA
FOR SITKA BLACKTAILS

There! Visible against the snow, just below a thicket on the opposite slope of a wide canyon, he stood looking over his back, neck swollen with the rut. Uphill, partially hidden in the trees, was a doe. In just a moment he would follow her into the alders and out of sight.

The wind was blowing off the mountain and toward the water, howling down the canyon from left to right. Uphill, with a strong crosswind, this would be a tough shot.

Months of planning and anticipation came down to that one moment in time. A split second's decision, should I take the shot?

THE SKY WAS CALM as the plane bounced in and out of the clouds. Below me I saw Kodiak's coastline with its narrow beaches, high cliffs, and ragged, mountainous interior. All was draped in white.

My first trip to Kodiak, I would be hunting with my friends Dana and Jarod Sorum for the next week. It was the island's Sitka blacktail deer, halibut, and duck we were after.

We de-planed and made our way to the terminal. The first thing I saw was a 1400-pound Kodiak brown bear on display.

It reminded me of what my friend Kevin Conway told me about hunting the island's deer. "Shooting a gun is like ringing the dinner bell. When

111

Dana Sorum glasses the beach from a boat on a Kodiak Island hunt for Sitka Blacktails. Gary Lewis photo.

you get a deer down, a bear is going to get a meal. Leave the gut pile, grab your deer and drag it away from there as fast as you can. Go fast and the bear gets to eat the gut-pile. Go slow and the bear takes your whole deer."

We were staying the week on the Deva, a 45-foot twin screw Tollycraft captained by Tom Mahoney of Joyce Marie Charters. We hunted during the day and returned to the beach in the afternoon, where Tom's son Abel would meet us to take us back to the boat, which was anchored offshore.

We worked toward the west side of the island to avoid expected storms to the east. There had been plenty of snow over the last few days. With the deer moving down out of the mountains we should find bigger bucks closer to the beach than at any other time of the year.

At 8:00 a.m. we were anchored in calm water in a small bay. After running all night, Tom had turned in. We donned wool pants and leather boots, and saw to our packs and rifles. It had warmed up to 35 degrees outside and a light wind was blowing.

Abel took Fred and Scott, two hunters with us from Spokane, over to the beach at first light. Several drainages came together in one place, feeding a small stream that emptied here into the bay. They would hunt up the hills to the left. Dana and Jarod would angle to the right, and I would go up the middle, climbing as high into the mountains as daylight and my own endurance allowed me.

Kodiak's drainages are choked with willows, devil's club, alder, and a few fir trees. As I climbed, I found fresh tracks and guessed we were pushing the deer ahead of us.

The higher I climbed the deeper the snow. At first to my knees, then it came to mid-thigh. Each step took effort, but I learned that some areas were easier than others. To get from one hill to another I had to walk between sidehills where the snow had blown away, and I couldn't always avoid the drifts.

I crested a hill and looked into a little valley, bisected by a small, willow-choked drainage. A doe—the first Sitka blacktail I saw—moved away on the other side of the trees. At every step she struggled in the deep snow. Through my glasses I studied her.

Small of body, she had short, upright ears and a short nose. Her long, winter coat was dark brown. A beautiful, graceful animal. I watched her crest the ridge and move over the other side. I followed.

I looked over the next hill and I saw no more deer, just trails in the snow, stretching out from bedding areas to feeding areas. Straight-ahead, trails cut around the tops of the hills and parallelled the willow stands. Escape routes. The deer were getting away from me without me seeing them.

I angled to the right and worked my way out onto a point and sat down, hoping to see deer moving away from my partners. I sat huddled against the wind, watching out over the valley and the beach below. I saw two deer emerge from the willows and I pulled my glasses to my eyes to study them. A doe and a fawn bounced through the snow. But this was the first week in December—the end of the rut. A buck could be following. I waited and watched.

Soon I saw another deer, a lone doe rooted in place below me in the alders. She looked up the hill, listening. Dana and Jarod were coming down toward her. She let them approach to within 90 yards then picked her way around them and disappeared into the brush. 🌿

Though two-man drives can be effective in Kodiak's forests, the preferred method for taking these blacktails is by spot-and-stalk. Much of the hunting consists of climbing to a suitable vantage point (of which Kodiak Island has no shortage) then glassing until a buck is spotted.

In open country, we found that the deer stayed one hill ahead of us, climbing ever higher as we struggled upward. In areas of thicker cover, they stayed in the brush, moving sidehill away from us or circling like a cottontail rabbit.

Deep snow changes the deer's movement patterns. They are then found at lower elevations—even on the beach, where they feed on kelp. As snow hampers a quick escape, they will often stand still or remain bedded, wait for the hunter to pass, and then sneak away.

A winter view of the Kodiak Island landscape. Gary Lewis photo.

WE FOUND THEIR beds hollowed out of the snow, beneath the low-hanging limbs of firs and downed alders. Their trails lead from bedding areas to feed, skirted the edge of meadows and creek bottoms, and stayed close to cover and escape routes.

Lunch was halibut chunks boiled in sugar and salt, dipped in melted butter and garlic. We ate pork roast for dinner and talked about the day. There were plenty of deer in the area, but the snow was keeping us from reaching them quickly or quietly. It seemed important to gain elevation but it was also apparent that, undisturbed, deer would be closer to the beach, feeding on bark and branch tips, grass and kelp.

I learned that these northern deer drop their antlers a lot earlier than the deer in the lower 48 do. In fact, they are known to shed antlers as early as the first and second week of December. We would have to be careful and use a neck rope to drag downed deer instead of pulling on their antlers.

I cleaned and oiled my gun and thought about the morrow. Armed with what I had learned, I resolved to move to high ground faster and quieter, then hook back toward the beach, still-hunting down from above.

We ate biscuits and gravy for breakfast then cruised toward the cape, watching the beach with binoculars for deer feeding at the water's edge. Shortly we began to see animals, but there were no visible bucks and not much cover to hold them.

As we neared the cape, the mountains moved back, stretching long fingers to the water. There were deer on the beach and I spotted another further out, just down at the water next to a rocky cliff.

I went ashore in the first boatload and ran along the beach. I found a trail near an old fishing cabin and climbed up the hill in the deep snow.

This time Dana and Jarod worked toward the mountains on the left. Fred and Scott went up the middle and I was on the right side.

It was colder—25 degrees with a stiff wind. I kept climbing, fighting the willows and the drifted snow. I climbed, stopped, glassed and climbed some more.

After two hours, I hadn't seen animals—only day-old trails in the snow. To my right, the land sloped away, draining into two other creeks separated by meadows closer to the water. This was the kind of undisturbed feeding and bedding area I was looking for. I turned and followed the sound of water beneath the snow—downhill.

Drainages converged and the brush thickened. I stayed on the right bank and watched the left. A lone buck saw me and moved off with his head down. Losing track of him, I tried to get a better look by working downstream, watching the thickets with my binoculars.

A doe and two fawns moved off then reappeared, watchful and curious at the edge of a meadow. I saw another deer skylined with head down. Moving over the crest, he went out of sight. Then I stood on a cliff above the water with the beach far below.

Dana Sorum with his Kodiak blacktail. Gary Lewis photo.

Seeing fresh tracks and beds everywhere, I worked back across a plateau. It was easier walking, with the snow only to my knees. Following the deer trails was quieter and faster. I came to another creek and crossed, coming up on the east bank, and paused to catch my breath.

There were two deer across the canyon and up the hill, almost 400 yards away. They stood on a trail entering a thicket of willows. The one in front had just entered the brush and I couldn't see her head, but the other was a buck. A big-bodied animal, he looked back at me, his neck swollen with the rut.

Through the glasses I could see his antlers were wider than his ears. On Kodiak that meant this was a good deer. It was too far to count points with my 7x binocular or 4x scope.

I sat back in the snow, snugged the butt of my Ruger 7mm Magnum into my shoulder and wrapped the rifle sling about my forearm, resting my elbows on my knees. Uphill, in the wind, this would be tough.

It was. In fact, I missed several times before I got the range right and waited for a dead spot in the wind. The buck was facing me head-on and I centered the crosshairs on his brisket and waited. Suddenly the wind was

Gary Lewis with his Sitka Blacktail from Kodiak Island. Best hunting on that trip was found in pockets of the heavy cover and browse. Gary Lewis photo.

still for a moment; I squeezed the trigger and sent my bullet across the canyon. I watched the deer through the scope. He was moving again, heading directly toward me, head down. He went through a patch of brush and came out the other side, crashing in the snow.

My hunt was over, but certainly not the thrill of it. I shook a little once the shooting was over. It was what I was there for—the long-anticipated moment. And once I rang the dinner bell, if there were a bear in the area, life would really get exciting.

I tied an orange ribbon to the spot where I'd made the shot and rested my rifle. Then I plotted a course through the canyon. I worked to one tree in a south-by-southwest heading then picked another and continued on a straight line to where the deer had gone down.

I found his tracks and followed them down the hill to where he lay, antlers buried in the snow. I quickly gave thanks for this deer whose meat would feed my family, then drew my knife. I needed to hurry. The afternoon sunlight was slipping away and Alaska's evenings are short in the month of December.

I set down my pack, coat and rifle, slipped my knife out, and moved to make the first cut.

All of a sudden something was coming toward me, rattling through the trees like a freight train. I heard rumbling, the ground shaking beneath my feet. I stepped back, away from the deer, ready to defend my life with my blade, if need be.

The ground rolled and I suddenly realized what was happening! It was an earthquake, not a bear attack. I breathed a sigh of relief and rode the quake out. Then bent to my task and worked quickly.

I had been warned. I was just a part of the food chain on Kodiak Island and not at the top of it. It was time to get this deer off the island.

I later learned that the epicenter was not far from where we were hunting. The earthquake measured 6.9 on the Richter Scale.

That night there was celebrating on the boat as we toasted our first success of the hunt. Though my deer tag was filled, I hoped I'd be able to watch Dana and Jarod fill theirs. I couldn't wait for morning and another look at Kodiak's deer.

December 7th dawned cold and calm. This was the third day of our Kodiak Island hunt. I had taken my buck the day before; now it was time to help Dana and his seventeen-year-old son Jarod beat the brush.

Moving single file through deep snow into the forest, we followed deer trails toward the mountain. We would set up a drive, hoping to push deer toward Jarod on the hill.

As he worked toward his stand, he too moved deer. A doe and a fawn sneaked away from Jarod and walked within ten yards of us.

When Jarod was out of the trees and above the scrub brush on the mountainside, Dana and I moved back to the beach. We headed west along the shore, about 60 yards apart inside the trees, staying in contact by the sound of our boots in the snow. Fresh trails and deer beds were everywhere in the thick brush. It was hard work. All manner of thorns clutched at us as we walked. Once I fell and grabbed a fistful of devil's club as I braced my fall.

I glimpsed movement and saw a deer to my left. Straight ahead, a fawn watching Dana was surprised to see me coming. A doe was between us and she headed out in a straight line along our backtrail. Dana saw a small buck sneaking away. After an hour we turned and headed back on a diagonal toward Jarod on the hill.

We had to cross a creek and a beaver dam—jumping across the opening where the water had breached it. The willows, elderberry, and alder were thicker now and the snow was mid-thigh deep. Sticker-bushes grasped at my coat. Every step was an effort, the tops of my legs burned with exertion. We fought through the brush seeking deer trails to follow, but there was no easy path.

I listened for the sound of Jarod's rifle. We were moving deer in front of us. I just hoped that one would be a buck. When I heard shots though, they came from behind us. Two rifle shots and then a third. I guessed it was either Fred or Scott (the hunters from Spokane).

Our efforts had moved deer near Jarod, but all he had seen were does and fawns. For over three hours he'd watched from his elevated position on the hill, huddled against wind and cold. We moved back toward the beach where Abel (the Deva's first mate) would meet us in the skiff.

Out of the alders at the water's edge, we stopped on a bluff and looked across the bay. The skiff was returning to the boat. Fred and Abel had a deer in the bow.

Fred had made a nice stalk and a long shot with his 7mm magnum.

His buck was a nice three-point with eyeguards. A fine looking deer of which he was proud.

Back in the boat, we motored west along the shoreline, seeing more deer in the sunlight on the forested hillsides.

Abel launched the skiff again, taking Jarod to the beach. A doe and a buck fed on the next hill. It was almost an island, surrounded on two sides by saltwater. A swamp cut it off from the mainland on the north.

As Jarod approached, the deer began to climb, heading for the safety of the trees on the crest. He watched the buck through his scope, hoping the animal would stop and look back. It didn't. It just walked out of sight into the trees at the top of the hill.

Hurrying down the beach, Jarod vanished from our view and circled the island. The two deer, seeking escape from the hilltop, ran toward Jarod and the swamp. Jarod shot and missed and the buck leaped the frozen water. Jarod chambered another round and waited for a good shot. When he saw his opportunity, he squeezed the trigger. The deer ran a few steps and went down.

Watching through binoculars from the boat, we cheered as Jarod emerged from the swamp dragging his buck.

There were still deer out feeding, so Dana headed out in the skiff. The sun was going down.

We watched bald eagles wheeling against the mountains, feeding on the beach and in the water. It was almost four o'clock and would soon be dark. The mountains were tinted with rose and gold from the setting sun.

Then we saw Dana coming back around the point. We cheered again. After looking over several deer Dana had filled his tag with a heavy buck. It had been a day to remember.

We anchored for the night in a shallow, protected bay. I spent some time before bed learning to identify harlequins, oldsquaw, and golden-eye. With four deer tags filled, we were going duck hunting in the morning. 🦌

Sitka blacktail are distributed in the coastal ranges along Alaska's south-eastern panhandle, Prince William Sound (good numbers on Montague and Knight Islands), and Kodiak Island. Biologists say they are descended from whitetail ancestors. Isolated in Southeast Alaska, they are a distinct primitive subspecies. At first glimpse, they are markedly different from mule deer, whitetails, and even the Columbian blacktail. Sitka blacktail deer have a brown tail with a black outline. As with whitetails, the Sitka's tail is often raised in flight.

His gait also distinguishes him from his relatives. He is a swift runner, but when he walks fast he often appears clumsy and uncoordinated.

Does and fawns are small of stature but bucks may be as large in the body as deer found in the lower 48. Their winter coat is long and thick, befitting a creature of the North.

Sitkas have a distinct double throat patch that sets them apart from other deer and their noses are short. Antlers are bifurcated like a mule deer's but a fourth point seldom develops. Mature two- and three-points with an average spread of 14 to 16 inches are representative of the species.

The ears of a Sitka blacktail average 15 to 15-1/2 inches apart from tip to tip. If you're looking for a mature buck, hold out for one with antlers as wide as his ears and at least half again as tall.

In recent years a number of non-typical racks have been taken on Kodiak Island. Many of these bucks are referred to as steer deer; sterile bucks whose antlers never shed their velvet.

Sitka blacktail are adept at using cover so binoculars are essential. When I hunted Prince of Wales Island we saw many deer in the lowlands. When startled, they ran for cover and often stopped behind an obstacle, only their face visible as they looked back through a screen of brush.

Bob Anderson, of Fireweed Lodge in Klawock, hunts deer in the high country on Prince of Wales Islands. On the tops of some of the highest mountains, the timber gives way to lush meadows. He says hunting for alpine bucks is akin to the spot-and-stalk methods used on Kodiak.

Whether you pursue deer in the rain forests of Southeast Alaska or on Kodiak Island, hunting the Sitka blacktail is an experience you will never forget. They are beautiful animals inhabiting unforgettable country.

A Sitka Blacktail doe on a gravel bar along the Harris River on Prince of Wales Island. Photo by Don Lewis.

Ed Park with his first Coues deer, taken on a hunt guided by Ollie Barney. Ed Park photo.

Chapter 9

TACTICS AND
TECHNIQUES FOR COUES DEER

By Ed Park

Most of us would celebrate if we shot a record-book buck, and probably become a record-book pain as we told and re-told the story—with appropriate embellishments of course. But ask Ollie O. Barney about the record-book Coues deer he got in Arizona's Santa Rita Mountains in 1965, and he'll hesitate. With prodding he'll tell the story, and although I've heard it many times, he always stays with fact. I know; I was there.

Ollie is one of the great old-time hunters and guides of the Desert Southwest. While he has a few animals in the record-books under his own name, he's mostly helped others bag trophies.

After Ollie helped me kill my first Coues buck in 1965, neither of us were eager to return to telephones and traffic jams, so I figured Ollie needed to fill his own tag. We left camp well before dawn—Ollie on his riding/pack mule and I on horseback—to hunt the rugged Squaw Peak country in the Santa Ritas.

Just as it got light enough to see well, Ollie suddenly reined up and pointed. High on the ridge a quarter mile north, two bucks were just drifting over the skyline. We only had time for a quick look with the binoculars—enough to tell that one was huge and the other larger.

We bailed off, tied our mounts, then hurried up the steep rocky slope, trying to avoid twisted ankles and all those thorny desert plants that kept grabbing at us. At the top we eased over the ridge crest to find ourselves looking directly into the sun, which was just then deciding it was time to get up. This produced miserable light flares on binocular lenses, but we studied the slope as best we could. Although the ridge was mostly open, there was no sign of those bucks. They'd simply vanished.

Then abruptly one buck just materialized and began feeding less than 100 yards ahead. For long minutes we searched for that buck's buddy. Ollie's puzzled expression asked better than words: *was this the larger one or the smaller one?*

The lens-flares were annoying enough, but another concern whispered its arrival as the warming dawn air began to swirl, gently brushing our cheeks. We'd be OK unless…

That fear was cut off in mid-thought as we felt a breeze on the back of our necks. Instantly that buck's head jerked up, nose working, and he began that alert, stiff-legged walk that meant study-time had run out.

Ollie's rifle came up and the desert air was shattered by the crack of his .243. As that buck dropped, another erupted from behind a small bush. We saw the most magnificent Coues whitetail rack I've yet to see. Ollie had taken the smaller one!

How small? Measurements showed it made the minimum record-book score. The one that got away was immensely larger.

Beside that evening's campfire we discussed what we'd change if we could rewind time and replay the morning. We would have backed off, circled to a new observation point, then kept glassing until we found both bucks and had the opportunity to assess them. Then Ollie would have planned his stalk.

However, there are dangers in passing up opportunities. Those fickle, scent-carrying breezes might have pushed both bucks into hiding. They might have abruptly remembered an appointment elsewhere, or other hunters could have spotted them. Taking the smaller might be better than risking getting neither.

On the other hand, serious trophy hunters must be willing to pass up the excellent in order to keep searching for the outstanding—and risk getting nothing. That's why it's called hunting.

That first hunt got me interested in Coues deer and I began studying. The Coues is a subspecies of our common whitetail deer, and sports the large tail and survival instincts of all whitetails. Because they are smaller, with correspondingly smaller antlers–and because their range is isolated from other whitetails–the Coues is listed separately in the record books.

Their range is southeastern Arizona, southwestern New Mexico, and northern Mexico. They are mostly found higher in those desert mountains than mule deer, and seem to favor elevations above 4,000 feet. They prefer woodlands of chaparral, oak, and pine, with interspersed clearings— although many are found on ridges whose main vegetation seem to be rocks.

That's about all the information you need for general hunting, but if the record-book bug bites you, you'll need higher education. Trophy hunting is not for everyone, but even those with little interest in record books will become better hunters by learning the techniques of serious trophy hunters. Seeing the outstanding trophy that eluded Ollie proved to me that such animals really do exist and triggered a new craving. I began seeking out other top hunters and learned that while they may disagree on some points of hunting techniques, they agree on most.

There is even a disagreement on how to pronounce Coues. Some say "cooz," while others favor "cows," because this deer is named after 19th-Century naturalist, Elliott Coues, who pronounced his name "cows." Nicknames, such as gray ghost, desert ghost and phantom fantail, attest to this diminutive deer's ability to hide where there is seemingly no cover.

Since Jim Shockey of British Columbia has taken all 30 huntable species/subspecies of North American big game with a muzzleloader (all 30 made the *Longhunter Society's Muzzleloading Big Game Record Book*), I asked his opinion of Coues deer.

He replied, "...these perfectly camo-ed hyper-sensory critters...are small enough to hide behind a shadow (and do) and they have the ability to shape shift. One second they are standing there, and the next second after you pull the trigger, there they are, still standing in exactly the same different place as they weren't before! No, it doesn't make sense to me either, but I'm not sure how else to explain all the times I've missed shots at these most wondrous of the deer species."

Most experts agree on the importance of scouting, knowing what you're looking for in terms of trophy size, hunting by spotting and stalking, and good shooting.

Scouting includes reading books and magazine articles; talking with others, including wildlife biologists, foresters, ranchers, taxidermists, and successful hunters; becoming intimate with the country via maps, hiking, and glassing; and off-season hunting for tracks, droppings, shed antlers, and the animals themselves.

To learn about trophy qualifications, read the various record books and haunt taxidermy shops to study antlers from all angles. There are several record books and every serious hunter should know them. The organizations that produce them address issues pertaining to wildlife management, hunters' rights, and the fair chase pursuit of big game, as well as providing record books that detail the largest-known specimens of each species (see chapter 3).

Although still-hunting or driving-and-standing take many deer, most serious hunters spot-and-stalk. Still-hunters mostly get running targets, so they must be skilled at shooting jackrabbits, because these little deer are seemingly not much bigger and every bit as tricky of a target. We've had little success with drives because, like all whitetails, Coues deer are highly skilled in the art of evasion.

Spot-and-stalk hunting is favored because hunters have the opportunity to study animals to see if they measure up to their desires. I got my best lessons from the late John Doyle of Tucson, who was recognized as both an outstanding hunter and a taxidermist. At his shop I studied antlers, while John pointed out the important aspects of main beam and tine length, number of points, mass, and uniformity.

Ollie Barney with the record book Coues deer he took in 1965. Photo by Ed Park.

Because hunting seasons are any taxidermist's busiest times, John began hunting before dawn, then quit in time to get back and open his shop on schedule. If he was late, customers knew he was busy packing out his own trophy from some desert canyon.

John hunted year around—but note I said "hunted," not shot. Since most Coues deer tend to live in a small geographical area for their entire lives, if a trophy buck is spotted one month, he'll probably be in that same area when the hunting seasons open. John was also an avid hunter of shed antlers for the same reason. If trophy sheds were found in the Spring, he knew that animal survived the hunting seasons.

Because of his scouting, John knew every situation within a logical drive of Tucson that provided north-south ridges and canyons. Well before dawn, he'd climb some east-facing ridge and ease over the top. Just below the crest on the west side, he'd find his pre-selected spot. He liked to be in position before first light to allow the desert denizens time to forget the intruder—and to enjoy the glories of another dawn.

On such west-facing slopes he'd be in full shade well after dawn, while the east-facing ridge to the west would catch the first light. When dawn brought it's golden wash to the ridge across the canyon, deer would begin drifting to their daytime beds—and John would see, and note.

When I hunted with John he pointed out every deer—buck or doe, large or small—and emphasized the importance of noting where each deer bedded, so they could be avoided. Many stalks have been ruined by a hunter bumbling onto a bedded doe he didn't know about. I was extremely impressed by how easily these desert ghosts simply vanished on an open rock ridge.

One critical aspect of hunting Coues deer is high quality optics. I begin with a binocular in the 7x to 10x power range. Avoid those with smaller objective lenses, such as 8x24, because while they're okay in bright sunlight, they're worthless at the end of the day when everything's in shadows. It's better to use a brighter binocular such as 7x35, 8x40, or 10x50.

For serious glassing I use a 20x80 Bausch & Lomb "big-eye" binocular. They're big and heavy, but that only forces me to use a tripod, which in turn allows detailed, hours-long study. For final trophy analysis I may switch to a 40x to 60x spotting scope, although I can see about as much detail with my "big eye" because of the binocular vision.

Coues deer can be hunted in Mexico, New Mexico, and Arizona. File photo.

Once your target is chosen, stalk to within range. Knowing where all other critters are is a key lesson taught me by John Doyle, as is the matter of scent-carrying wind direction. Beyond that, it's a matter of using the terrain, rocks, and vegetation to conceal your approach.

Chapter 16 has details on weapon selection for western deer, but a few Coues-specific suggestions might help. It takes a big Coues buck to top 100 pounds, so even lighter calibers, such as the .243, are adequate in the hands of a capable shooter.

The key word is "capable," and bullet placement is far more important than the numbers on the cartridge. The distance that shots are taken by spot-and-stalk hunters is determined by individual stalking ability. Those highly skilled in the art of close approach, don't need a 1000-yard, .50 caliber sniper rifle.

However, in the wide-open country of those desert mountains, a long shot could be your only option. In such cases, select a flat-shooting caliber in the .24 to .30 caliber range. I use a .30/06 and 150 grain Nosler Partition bullets.

Most Coues deer, and most record-book entries, are from Arizona. Of the 285 entries in the latest Boone & Crockett Club record book, approximately 80% are from Arizona, 14% from Mexico, and 6% from New Mexico.

For Arizona or New Mexico hunting regulations, contact their wildlife departments (see Appendix). Getting information for Mexico is difficult, but since most hunting there is on private ranches, thus requiring an outfitter anyway, simply let him handle the details. He knows the laws and procedures.

When John Doyle died, Dean Lippert bought the business, which is now Lippert/Doyle Taxidermy, 3232 East Ajo Way, Tucson, AZ 85713; phone 520-294-2637. Lippert is a good source for any Arizona hunting information, and also guides on several huge Mexican ranches that produce many Coues trophies.

To get more information about Coues deer, or guides and outfitters, check the Internet, but be forewarned: hunting phantom fantails can become addictive.

Gary Lewis at the end of a morning hunt for axis deer in Hawaii. Axis deer, also called chital, are native to Asia. They can be hunted in Hawaii and Texas. Gary Lewis photo.

Chapter 10

HUNTING AXIS DEER

SOME OLD HUNTERS have wondered if there will be deer hunting in Paradise. Hawaii isn't Paradise but it is pretty close to it. There is no other experience quite like hunting there.

We parked the truck and walked up the old Jeep road in the dark, finding cover beneath the spreading arms of a tree. Joey Joao, my guide on Molokai, settled into the tall grass and indicated where I should sit.

A pale glow appeared in the east and I could see the tops of the trees against the sky and hear birds waking to the new day. I smelled saltwater on the breeze.

To the north a turkey gobbled as it flew from its roost. It was the start of another deer hunt, just like so many other deer hunts—until a deer barked!

After six years of drought the winter rains of 2001-2002 had restored the green to Molokai's dry west end. On that morning, we were hunting axis deer on property owned by Molokai Ranch on Hawaii's friendly isle. 🦌

Axis deer were introduced to the Hawaiian Islands in 1868. Native to India, a small herd of the animals were a gift to King Kamehameha V from the Hawaiian Consul in Hong Kong. Initially they were established on Molokai. Subsequent herds were founded on Lanai and Maui.

Adult bucks stand three and a half feet at the shoulder and average 150 to 160 pounds. Females average 90 to 100 pounds on the hoof.

Their coats are golden brown, flecked with white spots from neck to tail. On throat and belly the hair is cream-colored. A black dorsal stripe runs along the spine.

Bucks grow unique, three-pronged antlers that can reach lengths of 30 inches or more in the main beam and over 20 inches wide. A hunter can always find these animals in various stages of antler growth. Axis deer breed throughout the year.

Hawaiian axis deer can be hunted on public grounds in March and April and on private land during the entire year. The elusive quality of the animal combined with its singular beauty and good-tasting meat makes the spotted deer from India a worthy trophy.

There are three types of deer hunts available on Molokai: Desert spot-and-stalk, rain forest ambush, and lowland scrub still-hunts. We hunted close to the ocean in broken country cut by runoff ditches and timbered with kiawe trees similar to southwestern mesquite.

WHEN THE DEER BARKED, I swiveled to the left with my binoculars. Joey spotted them first. The deer appeared like wraiths in the early morning light. "Doe and a small buck," Joey whispered. They approached within 60 yards then turned back into the trees.

Axis deer are nocturnal, feeding by night and bedding during the day. Grass and succulent plants make up the majority of their diet. Creatures of habit, they often take the same paths from bed, to feed, and to water. Where you see axis deer one day, you have a reasonable chance of finding them again.

We spotted the next group of deer about 150 yards away, crossing a fence, the road, and an open clearing. First came the does and fawns, then a few small bucks and one nice buck.

"There's a good one," I said. Joey was watching too.

"No. Too small," he said. "That's an average buck. Wait a little, we'll see a bigger one."

Then there were deer streaming by just 40 yards to our left. My head swiveled left and right, trying to keep track, watching for a big buck.

"There's one," Joey said. He pointed to a nice buck that had emerged from the trees and was trotting over the road and heading across the clearing

150 yards away. In a herd of does and fawns the big deer was safe. I held my fire, watching as it paused to look around. It was 200 yards out. No shot. The deer trotted into the trees.

The sun climbed higher. The turkey gobbled as it fed through the trees to the north. Behind us, another turkey gobbled. We watched and waited.

A fawn came out of the trees, slipped through the fence and crossed the road. She was followed by a doe, then another and another. Does, fawns, small bucks, and big bucks with small antlers, came through the clearing.

Another group of deer came out to our left and held up at the fence. They had sensed something was wrong and decided to cross higher up the hill. Joey tugged on my sleeve and pointed up the hill. He moved out to intercept them and I followed.

We set up in the shadow of another kiawe tree and waited. Nothing showed.

Joey guessed that the deer had moved higher yet, going around us. "Let's slip over the hill and see if we can find where they went," he suggested. Sounded good to me.

We slipped through the trees and I found myself looking into a dry creek bottom, probing with my binoculars. There! For a brief instant three deer were illuminated in the sunlight. I dropped to one knee, motioning Joey down. They were in there, feeding in the shadows. I saw parts of deer: ears, legs, backs, and spots. No antlers. But because I looked through the interlocking branches of kiawe trees, I couldn't be sure. I counted twelve deer, but saw no bucks.

On hands and knees I moved closer, looking into the creek bottom. For ten minutes, I watched the deer and waited for something to happen. Unknown to me, it *was* happening. From where Joey sat he could see a big herd moving down the slope to my left.

When the deer hit the dry creek bottom they turned right and headed straight for a pool of water trapped in a deep shaded hole.

A fawn and a doe moved through an opening just 35 yards away. I watched, looking for antlers. There were more deer coming. 150 yards away the other herd was filing out of the canyon and heading uphill toward their morning beds. I alternated between watching the near herd and the far herd.

Antlers! I saw a spike buck in the far herd and then a small hard-horned 3-point buck in the near group. Then I saw velvet antler tips in the near herd. The body of the buck was hidden by the creek bank. All I could see were the tops of his antlers, spaced about 24 inches apart. This looked like the buck I was waiting for, but I couldn't see his body.

I decided I would shoot when he came out into the open. The big antlers swiveled and headed back upstream. I guessed he would turn and follow the other deer through the opening. I waited, ready. Then I saw velvet antlers again as a deer came out into the open. I found the spot behind the shoulder, squeezed, and saw the buck turn.

Later, Joey told me that he watched two bucks run up the hill after my shot. One was the small hard-horn and the other was a bigger velvet-antlered buck. The one I had intended to take.

My buck traveled less than twenty yards before going down. Carefully I approached from the rear and saw the buck was dead. He carried a small three-point rack close to 20 inches high and a little more than 12 inches wide.

I had shot the wrong buck. I fell for the oldest trick in the book—the big buck sends the young buck out into the open first.

There was no disappointment, however. I had bagged my first axis deer on a hunt like no other. I'm looking forward to doing it again. ✦

Hunting axis deer in the wild is a worthy pursuit for any deer hunter. Their tendency to run in herds like elk, their vocal communication, stealth, and nocturnal nature makes them a difficult deer to harvest—even when they are found in abundance. The trophy hunter has an added challenge when he seeks to take a mature animal with outsize antlers.

Almost all mature bucks have three points per side. Most trophy hunters are looking for 30-inch or longer main beams. Like other deer, the ears can be used to determine the size of the rack.

Axis deer were introduced to Molokai in 1868. With no predators other than man, deer are numerous on Molokai and neighboring Lanai. Gary Lewis photo.

Ear length is four and a half to five inches. The brow tine should be one-and-half to two times the length of the ears. The second tine should be two times the length of the ear. Antler spread is not as important as symmetry, but for the sake of discussion, the distance between a buck's ears is 12 to 13 inches. Most good bucks have an outside spread of 18 to 30 inches.

Some axis deer use their tails like the whitetail, raised high while alarmed or in flight. When not feeling threatened, the tail is half-erect, tip pointed at the ground.

To hunt in Hawaii, you must show proof of passing a hunter education class. This must be done in advance through the Department of Land and Natural Resources (808-587-0200). The DLNR will send you a letter of exemption. Bring that with you to Hawaii to present when buying your license. The license can be purchased in person at a sporting goods store.

Hawaiian gun control is strict. Pay attention to the rules that keep you within the law and out of trouble. When you bring your own hunting rifle, check in with law enforcement within 72 hours of arrival. Be prepared to spend 30 minutes at the police station to fill out paperwork.

One of the most difficult aspects to hunting in Hawaii is finding access. For this reason, before you go, do advance research to find public land access. This should include phone calls to the DLNR office and law enforcement. For a first-time hunt, I recommend making arrangements to pay for trespass on private land or go on a guided hunt. Hard-horned bucks can be found any time of year, but according to local hunters, your best opportunities for seeing the largest amount of antlered-bucks are from March through May.

They are interesting animals to watch and to hunt. Their beauty and grace is unsurpassed. I was thankful to have had the opportunity to take one.

At the end of that Hawaii hunt, I found myself walking to the shoulder of the hill and looking out over the ocean. I sat down to watch the whitecaps and eat my lunch. The wind blew the taste of salt from the sea and a whale breached in the blue water. If there is deer hunting in Paradise, it will be a lot like that.

Chapter 11

HIGH ADVENTURE ON THE HIGH PLAINS

Hunting the Pronghorn

Why *is there a chapter on hunting pronghorn antelope in a deer hunting book?* Because pronghorns——worthy big-game trophies in their own right——are good training for desert deer hunters. In some western states exciting combination hunts can be made for pronghorns and mule deer .

Pronghorn antelope are unique to North America. At one time they rivaled bison for numbers on the Great Plains. But market and subsistence hunting reduced populations to the point where extinction was considered inevitable. Early in the 1900s, wildlife managers and far-sighted sportsmen teamed up to restore pronghorns to much of their native range and it worked. Hunters across the country are reaping the reward.

RAY SOHN BROUGHT the spotting scope into focus. A little band of antelope fed in the flat between two buttes. The animals were over a half-mile from where Ray, a roofing contractor and Tom Wills, his long-time hunting partner and gunsmith, sat on a rock outcropping.

Tom had spotted the herd a few minutes before. They had been feeding on the bunchgrass that grew in the bottomland. The antelope moved closer as they headed toward water. Ray focused on a buck whose horns were heavy and long. This was the buck he had waited 30 years for.

Ray had applied for his first pronghorn rifle tag in 1970, the year he graduated from Oregon State University. Under Oregon's old system, the odds were long, but he guessed that if he applied every year, he would eventually draw a tag. The law of averages didn't work in

Ray Sohn drew a long-awaited pronghorn tag and took this nice buck in eastern Oregon. Gary Lewis photo.

his favor. "After about fifteen years, I thought maybe I was filling out the application wrong, but I kept getting deer and elk tags." Though frustrated, Ray kept applying.

Meanwhile, his hunting partners drew pronghorn tags. The first year Ray's father (then 80 years old) applied, his name was drawn and he bagged a buck. Next, Ray's daughter, Elishah, was successful in the drawing and tagged her buck.

Finally, in 2000, it was Ray's turn. The day the notice came, he called Tom and went and bought his tag. The August hunt was planned.

The day before the season opened, the two partners were on the road early. By 8:30 A.M. they were in the hunt area. High on the mountain, they glassed four herds, finding one decent buck among them.

Later in the day they found a rock outcropping that overlooked a plain. There the vegetation was better and water was nearby. One nice buck stood out on a flat. Taking one look at the hunters, the buck vanished around the point of a hill and dropped down into a basin beyond.

From where Tom and Ray sat they could see seven different bands of pronghorns with between five and fifteen animals in each group. They were encouraged to see a lot of small bucks and numerous fawns among the groups. They saw does with twins and older does with horns. A healthy pronghorn population is composed of animals in all age classes.

When night fell, the hunters rolled out their tarp and sleeping bags beneath the stars. The desert sky was their ceiling. Coyotes sang in the distance.

Ray's hopes rose with the morning sun. There were bucks in the bottomland again but not the animal Ray was looking for. After 30 years of dreaming about hunting pronghorns, he wanted a trophy worth the wait. As Ray put it: "If I have to wait another 30 years, I'll be too darn old to hunt."

Remembering the basin buck from the day before, the partners went after him. Finally spotting him, they watched the lone pronghorn bed down. With a good idea of where to find him again, they headed up the mountain for one more look around.

From the point where they'd started early that morning, Tom took one last look. "There's a small herd out on that flat," he said. Ray looked through the scope and quickly forgot about the bedded basin buck. He saw another buck coming toward him whose horns were around fifteen inches.

They waited, Ray readying his Browning A-Bolt.

Finally the animals moved into the little draw below. It was a long shot, but one Ray felt he could make. Seated, he steadied his hand against the rock in front of him and settled the stock into his shoulder. 30 years of waiting came down to this. Crosshairs steady, he squeezed the trigger.

The buck's horns were indeed fifteen inches. Ray was more than satisfied as he admired his trophy. That meat was a high priority so, under the hot sun, Ray and Tom worked fast to remove the hide and cool the meat. 🐾

Some states have tight restrictions on the seasons due to few antelope. Tags are limited to draw-only so the hunt is of high quality with little competition from other hunters. Drawing a tag is a matter of applying year after year and having the patience to wait for your name to come up. These hunts provide the hunter with an unforgettable experience. He or she will see plenty of antelope and may blow several stalks trying to get close to a trophy animal.

In antelope-rich country, seasons may be longer and more tags available to more hunters. Your chances are less during the opening day of such seasons, thus less chances of connecting with a quality hunting experience. By waiting a week before heading afield, you'll find less competition for game. The animals relax and you'll have the great wide open to yourself.

A spotting scope is necessary if you want to take a trophy buck. You are looking for an animal with a horn length of 14 inches or better. The prong itself should be five or more inches long. Use the ears as a reference. The pronghorn's ear is about six inches long. If the horn is longer than two times the length of the ear, and the prong is almost as wide as the ear is long, you are looking at a good buck. If the width at the base of the horn appears to be half the length of the ear, you should be planning a stalk.

Pronghorns begin to establish their dominance early in the summer. They mark boundaries by pawing the ground and creating scent 'posts.' Does, seeking the best grass and cover, attach themselves to the dominant buck.

September's intensity is evident to the interested observer. The bucks with the best habitat control the biggest harems—numbering between six and fifteen does and fawns.

A buck is especially vigilant at this time as challengers to his domain wait on the fringes, hoping for a chance at a fling with a willing doe.

When a subordinate approaches, the herd buck must run him off. Fights are common and may last as long as half-an-hour—until one wounded and bruised animal limps away.

Spend a little time in pronghorn country and you can see the struggle played out time and again: an antelope buck standing watchful over his herd, while a smaller buck bides his time nearby, feeding, watering, and sleeping alone.

Good antelope country is not always good for hunting. Pronghorns stake their lives on their phenomenal eyesight. Raise your head and binoculars above the sage to study a barely visible distant buck, and you'll see him gazing back at you. On flat ground they are nearly unapproachable. Though capitalizing on their curiosity will sometimes enable you to get close. I found out a lot about antelope hunting on my first trip to Wyoming.

I'D DREAMED OF HUNTING in Buffalo Bill's backyard for a long time. After years of reading about hunting on the Great Plains, it was my turn.

Part of the allure of traveling beyond your home state to hunt is to participate in the legacy of our country. When you go hunting in another state, take time out to fish and tour a museum or a battlefield. There is so much to see and experience, so much history, that taking the extra time is sure to enrich your visit and the color of your memories.

In Cody, Wyoming we toured the Buffalo Bill Cody Museum, ate at The Irma Hotel, and took in a Western reenactment in the evening. Boots thumped on the boardwalk and spurs jingled at each step. The cowboy strode to the middle of the street and stopped, splendid in a black frock coat, broad-brimmed hat, and long mustache.

"We here in Wyoming still have our rights," he said. "You may have lost some of yours where *you* live, but out here in the west, we value our freedom and the Constitution for which our fathers fought and died. If you value the Constitution and the Bill of Rights," he went on, "Join the NRA, vote, and get involved in keeping this great country free."

In Cody, it's hard to escape the kinship of freedom and American history. Another big part of that history are the stories of the Indians, mountain men, and hunters of the plains.

Finally it was time to go hunting. The season had started a week earlier, but I waited, to avoid the hubbub of opening day. A week into the season I'd have the desert to myself.

After the show at The Irma, I took the family to our hotel and drove east into the desert. I wanted to see if I could find pronghorns. It didn't take long. On a long ribbon of road that cut through the sage, I found what I was looking for. The dust trails of a band of pronghorns. I would be back at daylight.

THE MORNING SUN WAS just a glow on the eastern horizon, a red ball of fire pushing back the desert night. I negotiated the hill in my Toyota 4-Runner and climbed to the top. The sky was dark blue and black sprinkled with stars in the clear September air. Framed against the blazing red-orange sun were three wild horses, their manes and tails blowing in the wind.

Less than half-an-hour later, I found the antelope.

The hunting rig is of immense importance in antelope hunting. It takes a lot of country to support these animals. You need to be mobile if you want to be successful—especially so if you are intent on taking a trophy. You may have to look at a lot of bucks before you find the one you want.

I was driving the top of a ridge when I caught a glimpse of movement to my left. There were eight in the band running past me. I slowed, watched them surge ahead, then followed. The road led me off the ridge and through a wash.

The antelope kept running down the ridge and out onto the flat. They slowed on a little rise and looked back. I parked about 700 yards away and watched them through binoculars out my driver's-side window. They also watched me. There was no way they were going to let me climb out of my rig, set up my shooting sticks, and take my shot. I had to think.

Then it came to me—a trick that I'd read about a long time ago. Make them think that you aren't interested.

I climbed across the passenger seat and slowly eased out the other side. Crouched below the level of the window, I slipped my Remington 243 out of the case and slipped cartridges into the magazine. I grabbed my shooting sticks, low-crawled to the back of the truck, and belly-crawled 50 yards from the rig before I stoood up.

Risking a glance backwards, eight pairs of eyes looked at me. I started to walk. Away from them. Slow and deliberate, I walked. Showing them that I didn't care. They watched me go, then drifted along with me. After two minutes, I made a hard left turn and angled back toward the herd. They watched. I drew closer, stalking them in plain sight. At under 300 yards away I stopped and carefully set up the shooting sticks.

The animal I would shoot stood broadside about 275 yards distant. I steadied the crosshairs, snicked off the safety, squeezed the trigger, and missed. Eight antelope turned and wheeled in the direction from which they'd come. Eight trails of dust burned out through the sage.

Another trick that some hunters use is to park their rig in full sight of the herd. If the herd stays still and watches the truck, the hunter can slip out the opposite side of the vehicle and crawl to within shooting range.

Walt Ramage, a pro-staffer for Primos Calls, shows off the Oregon pronghorn he took with his 243 and a Nosler bullet.

As I roamed antelope country, I began to look for rolling hills, washes, and valleys that would allow me to sneak within rifle range of an unsuspecting herd. I saw mule deer in the willows along the river and pronghorns in the sage. 🌿

Flat-shooting rifles such as the 6mm's, the .25-06, the .270, and 7mm magnum are the best choices for hunting these fleet-footed, thin-skinned animals of the plains. A 4x or 6x scope is right for most situations. Shots may be taken at long range in open country, so a bipod or shooting sticks come in handy. 8x to 10x binoculars are a necessity and so is a spotting scope if the hunter is looking to bring home a trophy buck.

Stalking may be done on hands and knees to get below the sagebrush, so the hunter's kit should contain protection from the cactus. I learned this quickly but was too late to do anything about it. While I pulled the two-inch cactus spikes out of my palms and knees, I told myself that next time I would wear kneepads and gloves.

Much of antelope country appears flat. But appearances can be deceptive. Look closer and you will find washes, gullies, and ditches that you can use for cover. Stream bottoms can sometimes provide cover. Trees, fence posts, sagebrush, and rocks can be all the cover you need.

I MADE ONE MORE STALK that ended in a lost opportunity. There was a herd of over 20 animals. One dominant buck with a lot to worry about. I made my approach from almost a mile away. Parking out of sight of the herd, I loaded my rifle and slipped into a dry streambed. It was deep enough that I was able to walk upright. The streambed led me down the river bottom for an eighth of a mile.

Leaving the river trail, I made my approach by crawling and low-walking up and over little features in the landscape. Rock piles, the foundations of old buildings, sagebrush, and run-off trenches allowed me to close the distance. Some trick of the wind gave me away. The animals were looking at me as I topped the last rise. They didn't stick around to find out any more.

My next chance came at the edge of a barren plain. I was driving when I spotted the herd. Again, curiosity was the key to my opportunity. I climbed out of the truck and laid down, making myself less of a threat.

The animal I wanted was on the far left. The herd ran, wheeled, stopped, and looked back. They gave me a fifty-yard shot. In the prone position, with my rifle at my shoulder, I found my target and squeezed the trigger.

I worked quickly to clean and quarter the animal before the heat of midday. The hunt was over. I felt thankful for this fresh meat, for the cactus spines in my palms and knees, for the freedom I enjoy, and this hunting heritage. 🌿

Spot-and-stalk hunting is the classical approach to antelope hunting. But sometimes special situations arise that force you to resort to other tactics. When other hunters—or your own efforts—have made pronghorns skittish, back off and watch them from afar. If you can monitor the animals from late afternoon to dark, you can be reasonably sure to find them in the same place at first light. Pay special attention to your surroundings, take a

GPS reading and return on foot, well before first light. Set up downwind and wait for dawn.

As with all other big game hunts, early mornings and late evenings are the best times to find antelope. The animals will be less wary as the sun is coming up. Cooler mornings and evenings generally mean a more predictable wind, which makes for better stalking.

If the animal you are after makes a dust trail for the state line, don't worry. Pronghorns are not nomads. They like their home turf. The herd will come back. A little patience can help you put some delicious antelope steaks in your freezer. Find a hide that will give you a clear view of a saddle, a wash, or a river bottom that the antelope might use to return. They will be back within an hour or three if you are patient. Keep your hunting rig out of sight, stay downwind, and keep still.

You can also follow fleeing antelope if the terrain will permit you to do so while staying out of sight. Chances are they fled over the next hill and settled down in a flat basin. Circle to get downwind and let them calm down before you stalk again.

On opening day (or any other time when there are a lot of hunters afield) you can use the activity to your advantage. Determine the likely routes of escape and post your partners in saddles between hills, or the dips between ridges, or on points of higher land that project into flats. Openings in fences and fence corners are also good places to set up for pronghorns on the move. Such places funnel animals and give you a better chance of catching a pronghorn on the run.

Know where the water is. Antelope need water like any other creature. Set up to watch natural travel routes to water.

Learn where the animals feed. Springs, seeps, and runoff may cause browse plants to grow greener and taller. Watch for those spots in an otherwise dry desert. There you will find antelope. (My Wyoming antelope was feeding on the edge of an alfalfa field. The herd bedded in the foothills, then watered and fed on the adjacent farmer's land. Such spots can pay off when you catch the animals moving from bed to feed, and back again.)

One more tactic that can work during the rut is to watch the does. If you find a herd of does without a buck in attendance, wait around. A buck will find them and stake his claim. Then you make your move.

Much of antelope country is flat, but pronghorns live in the badlands as well. The broken country makes for a beautiful hunt and you can use the terrain features to help you get close to the animals.

The key to good antelope meat is in the way it's handled after the kill. Heat is enemy number one. Temperatures in antelope country can climb pretty high during September. Go prepared to take care of your meat. A cooler, ice, a tarp, skinning and gutting knives, rubber gloves, paper towels, and garbage bags are essential.

Take your pictures, then gut your animal within fifteen minutes of the kill. Lay the animal on the tarp and begin skinning immediately. It is important to cool the carcass as soon as possible.

Separate the quarters. In morning and evening you can lay the meat where the breeze will start to cool it. Midday, lay the meat in the cooler on ice.

It is important that you keep the hair from touching the meat. Use paper towels to wipe hair off the meat cuts before bagging.

Our family eats nothing but wild meat. We all agree that properly cared for antelope meat is some of the best we have eaten. Take care of it.

Hunting pronghorns is an adventure like no other. Unique to this continent, they are an American success story.

Paul Coil with his daughter Katie on a Wyoming hunt. Katie used a 7mm-08 with a 140-grain Nosler Ballistic Tip. Photo courtesy Paul Coil.

Chapter 12

FOR MANAGEMENT, MEAT, AND MEMORIES

MERRILEE'S FIRST DEER was a mule deer doe.

"We'll skirt the base of that bluff in the shadow and come out on that little rise. You can take your shot from there."

We had split a herd of thirty animals earlier that morning and intercepted them again as we moved west along the creek. There were fifteen deer making their way along the brushy ditch. We saw through an opening in the trees.

If we used the terrain, I guessed we could close the gap and put Merrilee within range. But we'd have to hurry.

It was her third year hunting big game and she said it would be the last if she didn't get a deer within the next two days. It was my job to make it happen that weekend or my wife would cease to be my hunting partner.

We were hunting rangeland and alfalfa fields east of Oregon's John Day River. Weeks without rain had left the hills bare and dry. Few trees could be seen on the rolling landscape. The bottomland, though, was irrigated. Fields of cut alfalfa and pasture bordered the creek that wound through the valley. The green rectangles of irrigated land stood in stark contrast against the dry brown ridges.

As the morning light broke over the eastern horizon, we followed a fenceline to a pasture. Pheasants were waking to the new day and we could hear them rustling ahead of us as we worked through the chest high, dew-laden grass along a creek.

Merrilee saw them first. Mule deer bucks, does, and fawns feeding in the open fields between us and the black angus pastured to the east. There must have been 40 deer. The wind was blowing from them to us. Most were 400 yards away, a few fed closer. Dropping into the creek bottom, we could cover 200 yards and come up over the bank to take a shot. Could it be this easy?

Merrilee went first, carrying the .243 at the ready. We crossed the creek and made our way upstream, heading toward a fencepost that she could use as a rifle rest. Sneaking up over the edge of the bank, we looked out into an empty field. The herd had vanished.

Something had alerted them—maybe the sound of rocks rolling as we crossed the creek, a glimpse of us as we approached, or some back-eddy in the light breeze. Only two deer remained standing at the fence line. Merrilee said the 200-yard distance was too far to shoot, and I had to agree.

The inch-high alfalfa between us afforded little cover to close the distance. As we watched, they crossed the fence and disappeared into the meandering creek bed.

As the sun warmed the valley, we spotted other small groups of deer and made stalks on them, producing similar results.

It was finally other hunters that pushed the deer back toward us. We watched as twelve deer came over the crest of a hill and dropped into the alfalfa, moving straight toward us. From east and west, two smaller herds joined them. Through my binoculars I saw spikes, forked-horn bucks, and four-points accompanying the does. Merrilee would have to be careful not to shoot a buck, as her tag allowed her to take only antlerless deer.

With no brush to conceal us, we were visible and the herd split again. Half of them filed by to the east and the other half flowed west with the creek around a bluff. We set up at a fence line but again Merrilee chose not to shoot until she had a clear shot at a stationary target.

I remembered the other deer still in the valley. Hopefully they were feeling secure in the shadow of the bluff and the cottonwoods along the creek.

A trail at the base of the bluff provided access in shadow. We covered 100 yards without the deer seeing us.

There! 120 yards away, the deer moved in the field beyond the brushy creek bottom. A space between cottonwood trees provided a window for Merrilee to isolate a deer—to choose the animal she wanted.

A deer stopped in the opening and looked directly at us. "Now," I said. "Take a good rest and shoot."

She didn't need more prompting. This was the best opportunity she had seen in three years of hunting. She shot once, and then worked the bolt and shot again.

Later she told me she'd a hard time keeping the rifle barrel still. She wasn't sure, but she thought the deer had flinched at the second shot.

The herd streamed away up a dry hill, through the sage. Some lingered and looked back at us. But we had the duty to find if Merrilee's bullet had connected, to search for a trail, and maybe to follow-up on a wounded deer.

There was no need for that. Her second shot did the trick and her first deer was down.

Her face must have been a mirror of mine. I saw astonishment and relief, thankfulness and a touch of sadness. It was a good hunt. After three seasons of trying, it was her day. 🦌

Mention hunting for antlerless deer and you're likely to hear varied responses. Reactions may range from contempt for your ethics to applause for your herd management savvy. The truth is, that while antlerless deer hunting is sound management, it is also a way to add to your skills as a hunter. Best of all, it is good, clean fun and it never hurts to have that wholesome, fresh meat in the freezer. (I'm proud of all the deer I've taken. My first deer was a doe, taken with bow and arrow. Antlerless deer fill my memories and my freezer in between the bucks.)

In most western states controlled hunts mean that some years some hunters won't draw a tag to hunt for antlered deer. If you like to hunt, it makes sense to apply for antlerless tags as well.

When that magical day arrives when the drawing results are in the mailbox, I am just as happy to draw an antlerless tag as I am when I draw a buck

Jon Guenther with a mule deer he tagged on a ranchland hunt in Eastern Oregon. Gary Lewis photo.

deer or an elk tag.

A deer's job is survival. Every day, they must elude or outsmart predators. The doe is a worthy trophy for first time hunters as well as anyone who likes providing for their family from creation's bounty.

We hunt antlerless deer because a deer population that is allowed to grow unchecked is vulnerable to starvation when habitat is overgrazed. When deer congregate on winter range, natural food becomes scarce. Thinning is accomplished by allowing hunters to take antlerless deer. This prevents major crop damage and mass starvation.

It goes back to habitat. Any given area will only support so many deer. If the herd grows beyond the carrying capacity of the land, trouble is on the way. First, the land becomes over-browsed. Deer body size and quality diminish. Then along comes a hard winter. Starvation follows and deer numbers plummet. In the following years, over-browsed range supports fewer animals.

An antlerless harvest will consist of deer of all age groups. Though hunters know it is good management practice to take any antlerless deer during an antlerless season, some are afraid to take a buck or a doe fawn. It's understandable that a person would want to hunt full-grown animals. Here are a few good ways to increase your chances of bagging an adult deer:

Only shoot a deer that is standing or traveling with other deer. This helps you compare the size before you take the shot. Watch for the lead deer. It will be the one the other deer follow. Fawns don't lead herds.

Look at the snout. Adult deer have longer faces than fawns. Look for deer with longer tails. An adult doe's tail will be longer than a fawn's. If the deer are going away, look to see which one is widest through the body. Follow these rules and the antlerless deer you take will be one of the largest of the herd.

Many antlerless deer hunts are designed to reduce damage to private croplands. Removing a few deer from the fall herd will mean land-owners will see less crop damage during the following spring and summer.

Also, deer on private land are not as pressured as their public land counterparts. These deer tend to feed at more random times which leads to increased agricultural damage. The taking of a few deer has small impact on the grazing, but the remaining deer become more wary. Their instinct tells them to feed only when they feel safe—after dark.

For this reason, some of the best antlerless hunting is on, or adjacent to, private land. Access is easy to obtain when farmers are losing crops to deer. Understand though that this is for does, not bucks. Bucks have become a cash crop for many farmers.

ONE YEAR WE DREW two tags to hunt in the mid-October antlerless hunt. I called the district biologists and was given a list of the names of ranchers and farmers who had complained of deer damage. I picked a name from list at random and called.

"Well," said the man on the other end of the line, "I guess you'd better come out." Come out we did. For fifty dollars, we rented their guest house and in the morning had to travel less than half a mile to hunt. We each bagged a doe. 🌿

I like to arrive early enough the day before the hunt to get a feel for the land. I look at the way the ridges run, find out where the water is, and look at the hilltops.

Again, look for the places where deer bed. Benches, with slope to the back and a commanding view to the front, give deer a sense of security. With rimrock to their backs or being one ridge removed from man, deer feel safe. Saddles are the natural travel routes from one valley to the next.

Farmland is almost always fenced. Walking fence lines gives you a clue to the travel routes of the herd. Crossing points will be evident from the deer hair snagged in the barbed wire.

Deer usually drop down out of the hills in the evening to feed in the fields at night. In the morning they return to their bedding areas. Set up along their travel route for a shot.

Taking a deer from a herd is not always as easy as it sounds. They seem to know the range of a rifle. Seldom will the herd allow a hunter to approach within reasonable rifle range. Pay attention to the wind when planning your stalk or your ambush. Use all available cover to get close. Remember, in a herd of 40 deer you have to beat 80 eyeballs.

Why do I hunt antlerless deer? Because I am, first and foremost, a deer hunter. There is little else that I would rather do than watch a herd of deer through my binoculars, then try to get close by watching the wind and staying out of sight. The pursuit of a deer shouldn't always be about antlers. Let it be about the land, the companionship, the animal and the hunt.

Chapter 13

THRIVE IN
THE BACKCOUNTRY

Hunting Gear and Survival Skills

WHAT TO CARRY WITH YOU

Hunters have always placed a certain amount of faith in the items they bring on the hunt.

When an Indian went hunting he carried his supplies and dried meat in a rawhide bag worn over the shoulder. Today we call it a backpack. The Indian also carried a smaller pouch slung over a belt. In it he carried flint and tinder for making a fire. Today's hunter calls it a fanny pack. Any hunter knows that survival equipment is as important as any equipment he carries into the woods.

As critical as regular shooting practice is for the bowhunter, bringing the right gear might be even more important. In a survival situation, a simple item like a space blanket or waterproof matches can mean the difference between dying of hypothermia and just spending an uncomfortable night in the woods. But space is limited and extra weight drags you down. So what *do* you bring?

A compass and map should be in your survival gear. If you're hunting unfamiliar country, you need quick access to your compass. Use it on the way in and on the way out. Trust your compass even when it goes against your 'sense of direction.' (Trusting my compass has helped me out of a lot of situations where trusting my sense of direction would have only helped me get lost.)

A compass is mandatory, but a GPS unit is a good idea. Use it in conjunction with your compass and map.

Almost as important as your compass is a light. Don't be without one. I carried a Mini-Mag flashlight and extra batteries for years, but have recently found a way to do without them. It's an innovation called the Photon Micro-Light II. Using a lithium battery, this little marvel is the size of a quarter but produces light that is visible for over a mile. It has a white light that is brighter than a flashlight ten times its size.

If you have to stay out overnight, having the means to build a warming fire is important. Not only do I carry waterproof matches, I carry a lighter and dry tinder. If I have to build a fire, I want to be sure I'll get it started.

A space blanket is another necessity. Folded into a package about the size of your wallet, this little item along with a fire could make a dark, lonely night a little more comfortable.

Next on the list is energy bars. I always carry one in case I get lost. There are plenty on the market to choose from. One of my favorites comes in carrot cake flavor. Sometimes I get lost just so I can have an excuse to eat it.

A length of leather thong or parachute cord can come in handy. I like to carry at least four feet of cord.

If I need to mark a trail, I always have plenty of surveyor's flagging in my fanny pack. Just remember to take it down on your way out.

Rubber gloves are nice for field dressing game. They take up little space in the pack.

In dry country you should carry water. I like to have at least 32 ounces per day while hunting. I put one canteen in my fanny pack and carry another in the backpack. If I leave the backpack somewhere, I still have water with me. Carry a water purifier where there are springs or streams you can drink from. Any backpacking supply or sporting goods store will have a good supply to choose from.

Depending on your style of hunting, a first-aid kit, laser rangefinder, moccasins, a spare bowstring, camouflage face paint, extra release aids, a broadhead wrench, and a predator call might find a place in your fanny pack. Hunting is a highly personal sport, so gear is a matter of preference. Take time to think it through, and pack gear you would need if you lost your way.

In the wilderness, an unexpected snowfall or a flash flood can change plans in a hurry. Preparing for an emergency will help you deal with trouble if it finds you. In a survival situation you will need four basic things: food, water, first aid, and shelter. A few items packed in a daypack or fanny pack may help save your own life or that of another.

Wilderness weather comes

Dan Turner and Kurt Christopher on a backpack hunt in Hells Canyon. If something goes wrong, preparedness is the key to survival in the wilderness. Gary Lewis photo.

in extremes. You may find yourself lost in a new area, stranded in the snow, with a broken ankle, or bleeding with a deep cut from your own knife. Accidents happen. Be prepared for anything and keep the will to survive.

Stock your survival pack with careful forethought. A half-day hunt won't take you far from roads, so minimum survival gear would be required. A seven-day pack-in hunt will lengthen rescue time. Multiply survival gear accordingly. Be prepared to rely only on yourself.

A positive attitude may be the most important factor to keep yourself from succumbing to the elements. You are probably the only one you can depend on. Wishing that another person was there to help you will not do any good. Hoping that another hunter will happen along won't make it so.

Spend some time before hunting season learning about how to handle severe cuts and broken bones. Being prepared with the right supplies will help. But your survival—or the survival of your hunting partner—may be ultimately up to you.

Osage Indians, going on a long hunt, often carried a bundle that contained a hawk skin. Looking on it was supposed to rekindle the courage of the warrior. Today you could get in trouble for carrying around a dried hawk skin, but you can take

Gary Lewis fills his Seychelles water filter on a summer scouting trip for blacktail deer.

courage in knowing that your survival pack is stocked with all you need.

HOW TO BUILD A SHELTER

Sometimes there is no way around spending a night in the woods. In most cases, you won't have a sleeping bag or tent with you. You have to make do with what you have in your survival pack or day pack. When you determine there's no way that you can find your way out before dark, resign yourself to roughing it and make camp before nightfall.

You can do without food, you can do without water, but you must have shelter to keep from growing hypothermic during the long, cold night.

If you have a plastic tarp, a space blanket, or a poncho, you're ahead of the game. If you're without those items, you can still spend the night in reasonable warmth if you keep your head and build a shelter.

The most important thing is to stay calm. Remember, millions of people over thousands of years, have spent unplanned nights outside and survived. So can you.

Pick a spot where you can find shelter from the prevailing wind: in the lee of a boulder, a fallen tree, or a cliff. Using tree limbs, build two more walls in the shape of a lean-to to shelter you, your bed, and your fire from weather. Make a thatched roof of pine or fir boughs over your head. If you have a plastic tarp, lay boughs on top of it to keep out rain and snow.

Gather as much dry firewood as you can find. Get more than you think you'll need. In the middle of the night it may be necessary to restart your fire. Keep a stack of dry wood close.

Build your fire against a boulder or a stack of logs. As much as possible, direct the heat inside your shelter where it will do the most good.

Hollow out a depression in the ground for a bed. Line it with needles or leaves and stack a pile of boughs nearby. When your fire is burning bright and your day is done, you can pull the boughs over you and keep hypothermia at bay.

HOW TO FIND YOUR WAY OUT

If you lose yourself in the woods without a compass or map there are some easy rules to remember to help you find your way.

Stop and think, resolving not to panic. Listen. A vehicle traveling along a road some distance away may give you a reference point to travel toward. Climb a tree or a hill and look for signs of civilization such as roadbeds, buildings, fences, or logging areas.

Without a view of a place to head toward, find a stream. Water will always flow toward a larger body of water. Camps, houses, and towns are built near water. Following a stream will always eventually bring you to civilization. When you cross a road or trail determine whether it's being used. Move along that road or trail until you come to a fork. Which one is the main trunk of the road? Most roads branch as they leave civilization. Turn away from the fork and head back along the main road toward help.

Moss on trees and boulders can also tell directions. Moss grows thickest on the side that faces north.

You've heard that people lost in the woods tend to travel in circles. To keep yourself from doing that, pick out a tree and walk toward it. When you reach the tree, sight along your backtrail and then extend it in a straight line toward another landmark. This will force you to move in a reasonably consistent direction and avoid wasting energy.

Survival, after all, is up to the individual. It costs little money and time to be prepared. It can cost you your life if you're not.

USING A COMPASS

It doesn't take long to get turned around when there are no landmarks. And relying on your own internal compass is a good way to get even farther off course.

All travel requires some type of navigation. Start by spending time at home, poring over maps of the hunt area. Try to picture the lay of the land by picking out landmarks.

Navigating in the backwoods is easy to learn and usually does not have to be precise. However, in the event of an emergency involving a member of your party, you must be able to find your way out by the quickest way possible, describe the situation to a rescue team, pinpoint the exact location, and be able to direct or lead help back to the injured person.

Those of you who use Global Positioning Systems stay with me. Technology *can* let you down. You should still bring a map and compass as backup. Many GPS units will fail in deep canyons or heavy timber. And batteries do run down from time-to-time.

Most people are not intimately familiar with the places they hike, hunt, or fish. But you don't need to be to find your way from one spot to another and back again. You just need to follow a few simple guidelines.

Bring a good compass. It doesn't need to be expensive but it should be reliable and of the protractor type with a dial that can be rotated 360 degrees.

Carry maps of the hunt area with you. Use your compass when you leave camp. Note direction of travel and refer back to your compass when you change course.

Try this exercise. Stand holding your compass and note in which direction the magnetic needle points. This is magnetic North. Orient your map so that the North arrow points in the same direction as the compass needle. Place the compass on the paper with the edge of the instrument along the intended line of travel. Then turn the dial until 'N' points to north. Note that the direction in degrees is read at the index line of the dial.

Declination is the difference between magnetic North and true North. Make the adjustment recommended on the map for the area you are in. Compensate for declination by rotating the dial the distance indicated on the map legend.

Next, pick up the compass and hold it level so that the needle is free to rotate. Turn your body until the pointing-end of the needle aligns with the orienting arrow and 'N' on the dial. Sight along the direction of the travel indicator and pick out a distant landmark, whether it be a tree, a rock, or a mountain. Proceed to your landmark and pick out another one from there. Follow this pattern until you arrive at your destination.

USING A GPS

A Global Positioning System receives and interprets signals from satellites in orbit above the earth. At any time, at almost any place, a handheld GPS unit can tell you exactly where you are. Of course, if you're already lost when you consult your GPS for the first time, you won't benefit too much from having a machine confirm it. But if you—prior to getting lost—establish a point to return to, then you can easily use the machine to find your way back.

The Global Positioning System was originally developed for the U.S. Department of Defense as a highly accurate navigational and targeting system. They lock on to high-frequency radio signals from some of the satellites in orbit and calculate through triangulation the exact location of the hand-held unit. At any time, a hunter can set and mark points along the path that he might want to return to.

Once, on a deer hunt, I found a spring burbling clean cold water. I marked it as a waypoint on my GPS. After we killed and packed out a big buck that day, we were able to (with confidence) find that spring again and refresh ourselves before walking out to the truck.

A GPS unit is much more than just a high-priced compass. For instance, a hunter pining away for snow to melt can sit at his dinner table and plot out the latitude and longitude of a high mountain meadow he wants to scout. By entering the coordinates into the GPS unit, he can hike

A bicycle gives the hunter quiet access to forest roads for pre-season scouting trips.
Photo by Tiffany Lewis.

straight to it in the spring just by following a course set months earlier in the comfort of his home.

Similarly, a bowhunter scouting in mid-summer can pinpoint the meadow where he wants to be on opening day. Then, instead of stringing orange flagging all over a mountain before the sun comes up, he can just return to the original waypoint using the backlit screen.

A friend once told me of the time when, after much scouting, he found a meadow loaded with elk sign. It was definitely the place he wanted to be when the season opened. Setting a waypoint, he returned to his truck and started driving roads, watching the digital readout until he found the spot where he could park closest to the meadow. On opening day he was back there with just a minimum of effort.

It should be stressed that a GPS won't get you out of the woods when your only set of batteries dies. And satellite contact can be lost in dense cover and deep canyons. Be sure to have extra batteries and a good map and compass as backup.

HUNTING ALONE

Some of my best hunting memories are of the trips I made by myself. Etched on my memory are the quiet times in camp with the stars looking down while I ate a late dinner, or the hours spent dragging harvested game to the road. There is satisfaction in going alone, in the scouting, in the contemplation, in discovery. When you notch your tag and finally reach the road with your burden, you feel a great sense of fulfilment.

The down-side of hunting alone is the risk that, if you are injured out there, you may not make it back to civilization. A few precautions are important before heading out on your own.

Tell someone where you're going. Leave written instructions with your spouse, your neighbor or a relative, describing where to go, where to look and who to call if you don't return by a pre-arranged date or time. If your plans change, check in with them to let them know you are headed in another direction.

Bring a cell phone. You may not get cellular service in your remote canyon honey hole, but cell signals can be received on the tops of many mountains across the West. Just leave it turned off. My friend Ryan Eicher once had his phone ring as he was getting ready to squeeze the trigger on a mule deer buck in the Cascades. The deer didn't wait around to see who was calling.

If possible, leave GPS coordinates of your camp with your contact back in civilization. Bring a GPS with you, as well as a map and compass. Make sure you know how to use them before you leave home.

Pack your survival gear. If you have to spend a night in the woods, a tarp or space blanket can save your life. A fire, energy bar, and extra water can make it more bearable.

In a culture where so much is done for us, in a country where wild places are being swallowed up by cities and suburbs, how do we maintain the spirit of adventure, rugged individualism, faith, and the 'can-do' attitude of our ancestors? By hunting.

Meriwether Lewis, Daniel Boone, Jim Bridger, 'Broken Hand' Tom Fitzpatrick, Jedediah Smith, Buffalo Bill, and Theodore Roosevelt were but a few of the men whose life stories I devoured when I was young. One thing that each of these men had in common was hunting. These were the people who were willing to risk their lives in pursuit of fortune and adventure. They hunted, trapped, and fished to live. Along the way they opened up a country.

The common thread that runs through the fabric of their lives is their willingness to abandon security and risk their very existence to pursue a dream.

Risk is inherent in hunting. As you pursue this way of life you may be stalked by a mountain lion, mauled by a bear, or lose your way in the mountains or desert—thereby increasing the odds of coming home with a great story to tell, or not coming home at all. Still, it is the risk-takers in our society who achieve.

What does all of this have to do with hunting, and why is it important to keep hunting in our culture? It binds us to our roots, to a time when men and women sought their own way in the world with little more than desire, a thirst for knowledge, and faith to sustain them.

Chapter 14

DEER CAMPS

On Your Own or With a Guide

When I took journalism in high school we were taught to answer six questions: Who, what, when, where, why, and how?

In hunting magazines, much is written about what to hunt when, where to go, why we hunt, and how we do it. Little emphasis is placed on who. Yet *who* we go hunting with often makes the difference between a trip to remember and a trip to forget.

Have you ever returned from vacation, excited to go back to work because you needed a vacation from vacation? Hunt with the wrong party and you will feel the same way. In fact, I know some people who have taken a permanent vacation from hunting because they were so burned by the experience.

Who cooks the meals? Who washes the dishes? Who cuts the firewood? Who gets first shot? How is the meat divided? These questions and more need to be asked when you start putting together a deer hunt. No *one* person should be left with all the work.

Most people hunt with their families first. Children learn from parents, uncles and aunts, or grandfathers. Sometimes a neighbor will offer to accompany a child through hunter education and then take them hunting. Children are thrilled to go afield with anyone who'll take them!

After a few years of hunting, you learn to take more responsibility for yourself and accept the burden of putting together your own party. If you're careful, you can put together a hunt made up of the type of people you can get along with.

You want to go with people you can depend on to be on time and honor commitments. I cannot count the number of times that hunting partners have backed out on me after months of planning. When something is as important as a hunting trip, it hurts to be let down at the last minute. The best defense is to plan the trip yourself or make contingency plans if the party leader backs out.

When I look back over the people I have hunted with since I was a kid, I can identify ten different types of hunters, both male and female.

Don't let "Jealous Jake" in your camp. Jake is a pessimist and a whiner who complains about the weather, the hunting, and the game commission. Take a bigger buck and you will get the cold shoulder and whispers behind your back.

"Billy the Braggart" is welcome. Somebody has to be the entertainment. I like listening to his stories. I'll let Billy stretch the truth a little if it suits his tale, but he must know how to shut up once in a while so someone else can talk.

I like to have "Ned the Novice" in camp. He hasn't hunted much, if at all, but likes to read about it. He listens to Billy the Braggart with rapt attention, and is willing to learn. The last time I camped with "Ned," he was one of two in our party of eight who took an elk. Unfortunately, his enthusiasm was dampened by Jake's mutterings.

"Ernie the Eager" is one of my favorite companions. He is always willing to climb another hill and look into the next basin. On the fifth morning of the hunt, he will be up making breakfast while the rest of us pretend we didn't hear the alarm clock.

"Well-fed Fred" likes to hunt and has a few seasons under his immense belt. The trouble is, he can only get two hundred yards up the trail before lunchtime. When you go afield with Fred, make it easy for him, and plan to hunt close to camp.

"Know-it-all Norman" might be the most difficult. He wants to try a different area because there's more game there. His compound bow is the best because the company who made it says it is. His truck is better than your truck because he subscribes to *Consumer Reports*. Get Norman to complain about the food! Since he knows more about camp cooking, make him head-cook and dishwasher.

"Clueless Carl" could get lost in a paper bag. He has never taken the time to learn how to use a compass. He doesn't come to camp with a map of the area. Carl is secure in the knowledge that someone else will take care of him. Get Norman to take him under his wing.

"Alcoholic Al" is dangerous because you never know how he will act under the influence of the liquor he sneaks along in his duffel bag. He drinks to deaden the pain of some distant memory, and his moods range from morose to moronic, from hysteria to hilarity. The drink also deadens his good judgment. Don't stay in camp with someone who mixes guns with alcohol.

Worst of all is "Oliver the Outlaw." Sometimes he masquerades as Billy the Braggart, Jealous Jake, or Ned the Novice. Watch closely and you will see him for what he is. He may come to camp without a license, or he carries someone else's tag. After he bags his game, he keeps hunting with the intent of taking an animal for someone else. The Outlaw complains about the game commission while he tries to justify poaching. Hunt with such people and you will be stained with their reputation. You might even get to ride in the back of a police car with them.

When you make your plans for next season, take a hard look at your would-be hunting companions. Take a look at yourself. Who are they? Who are you? Who will you all be on the sixth day of a week-long hunt?

If I could pick only one type of person to hunt with the rest of my life, it would be "Leather-skin Larry." He's the one I can depend on in grizzly country—someone I can trust with my life. Larry is often very picky about who shares his camp. You should be too!

HIRING AN OUTFITTER

THERE WAS A PRETTY GOOD CROWD at the sportsman's show. I had pushed my way up to the edge of a table advertising hunting and fishing trips from Mexico to Alaska. I had the attention of the guy behind the counter and was leafing through his photo album, looking at pictures of some of the massive moose his hunters had taken over the last couple of years.

Next to me, a guy my age reached into his wallet and took out a Visa card. The booking agent excused himself to talk to his new client. A winning smile, the position of his display, quality of his pictures, and decoration of his booth won another client who might as easily have booked his trip with the competition on the next aisle. 🍂

Outdoor shows are where many fishing and hunting guides book most of their new business for the year. You get there early on a Saturday, push your way through the crowd, look at the photos, run your fingers through the hair on a bear pelt, and soon you're imagining yourself still-hunting down some forest trail in the north country, or waiting in a duck blind at first light, or hip-deep in some Alaskan stream casting a marabou streamer to sockeye salmon.

Six or seven months later you board a plane or drive your car to some remote destination you've never seen before. You have invested more money than your spouse thinks you should have and you are excited. But one little question nags at the back of your mind. The same question on everyone's lips when they greet you upon your return: "How was your trip?"

Will it be everything you imagined it to be?

There *are* steps you can take to ensure that your trip across the state or across the country will be successful—whether or not you take a trophy buck or catch a 40-pound salmon.

The first step in planning your big fishing or hunting trip is to decide who you want to spend all that time with. What can you expect from your regular partners? Are they the kind of people who will keep their spirits up when the rain falls for four days straight and much of your time is spent

Nick Mosich (left) and Gary Lewis with two bucks they took on a hunt in Idaho's Gospel Hump Wilderness with Shepp Ranch guide, Jeff Bruce. Gary Lewis photo.

trying to keep dry? Are your goals for the trip compatible? You should hunt with people with similar expectations.

And ask yourself will you be satisfied if you see a few animals but never get a chance at a trophy? Will you be pleased if the only fish you catch is a 30-pound halibut when the guide's literature promised a 50-pounder or better?

Be equally careful with *who* you book your trip with. When you buy a hunting or a fishing trip, ultimate success is not guaranteed. You're still subject to the same variables you experience closer to home. It could rain the whole time and blow out all the rivers, or an unseasonable snowstorm might drive the deer to lower elevations. Be careful if the outfitter assures you that you will bag your buck or limit-out on steelhead. Real life does not always work that way.

Ask the outfitter what you can expect of him and his crew, and let him know what he can expect of you and your partner. Will you be expected to haul water, chop wood, or feed the horses? How will the hunt be conducted? Does the guide prefer to push the brush, use spot-and-stalk methods, or put you on a stand in the morning and come pick you up again after dark? Will the guide butcher and pack out your elk? Can you keep a few coho to bring home or will all the fish be released?

Also ask about the previous year. A prospective client has the right to know if a severe drought or a hard winter took a toll on wildlife and fish. And don't book your hunt until you have contacted the outfitter's references at random. Don't just call the ones he gives you first, ask to speak to people who went home without filleting a fish or bagging a buck. When you call the reference, ask about the guide's ethics and ask if they would book a trip with that outfitter again.

Once you think you've selected your outfitter, find out one more thing. Contact the Fish and Wildlife department in the state or province where you intend to hunt. Ask them if outfitter and guide services in that state or province are required to hold licenses to conduct business. Is your outfitter's license current? Be aware, some state laws say that hunters using the services of an unlicensed outfitter or guide may be held in violation.

Adam Brooks works breakfast magic on a scouting trip for blacktail deer.
Gary Lewis photo.

Get in good physical shape, make sure you bring the right gear for the weather you could experience. Going hunting? Then practice shooting under the conditions and at the distances you will encounter in the field. When you finally arrive at your destination, go at it with all the enthusiasm you have mustered over the long months of winter and spring.

Be cheerful, stay out all day and listen to your guide. You paid him hard-earned money to make your stay worthwhile. The attitude you take with you will help create the memories you bring back home.

IN 1999 I MADE CONTACT with a company from Alaska. I had never heard of the outfit before, but the pictures they showed suggested that I book a trip with them to the cold, windy passages of Kodiak Island. After calling the references they gave me, I did. I will never forget the experience of hunting that frozen land and fishing its narrow fjords, hiding in sheltered coves through the long winter nights. 🍁

That was the good side of buying a guided hunt. Now read the story of a man who saw the other side:

He had always wanted to pursue black bear in British Columbia. After saving his money for the trip, he booked his dream-hunt with a Canadian guide. He spent the following months getting into shape.

Fully-outfitted, the adventure began in the Canadian bush. From base camp, they would prowl river bottoms and hunt old logging operations looking for black bears.

Unfortunately, base camp proved to be a back room in the guide's house. The client had to buy food for the guide's family. Transportation was a broken-down pick-up. The guide, who appeared to know nothing about hunting bears, was surly—as well as a dangerous driver. The client found these things out all on the first day. The adventure went downhill from there.

QUESTIONS TO ASK WHEN BOOKING A WHITETAIL HUNT

1. Is there a game fence?

2. How many acres are behind the fence?

3. Is the fence designed to keep deer in or keep deer out?

4. Is artificial propagation practiced?

5. Is a license required to hunt?

6. Are animals trucked in to replace animals that have been taken by hunters or is the population self-sustaining?

7. What methods do guides employ to put hunters in front of game?

Too often, a well-polished smile, a colorful display, some antlers or fish, and full-color photos are enough to convince unwary sportsmen to part with their money.

The outdoor shows are where fishing and hunting guides book their new business for the year. You push your way through the crowd and page through a stack of photos. Pretty soon you can imagine yourself stalking caribou on the tundra or standing in a glacial river with a big chinook salmon tearing line off your reel.

Eight months later you board a plane. You invested more cash than your family thinks you should have and you're excited. *Will it be everything you imagined?* You can be more confident of the answer if you ask the right questions in advance.

When you go to book a guided hunt, don't check your dreams at the door; but do remember to do your homework first.

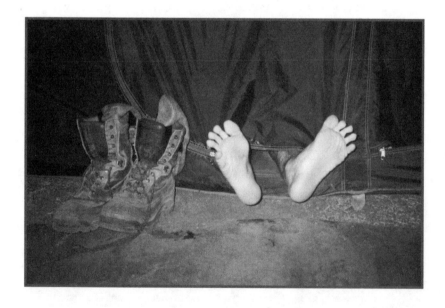

Chapter 15

PREDATORS

As stewards of the resource, and as the ultimate predator, our role in nature is to keep animal populations in balance. We control deer numbers to limit the large fluctuations in populations that can strip an area of its browse and hurt the carrying capacity of the land. Similarly, predator control seeks to simply keep populations in check so prey species are not impacted.

Hunting predators can add an extra dimension to your deer or antelope hunt. Coyotes can be found across most of the west. In Alaska the deer hunter may encounter wolves, illegal to hunt in that state. In many places, black bear and mountain lion tags can be purchased at the same time as the deer tag.

For the deer hunter, predators are a bonus, a target of opportunity. The extra expense of the tag just might be offset by the thrill of bagging an unexpected trophy.

A FEW YEARS AGO, I hunted elk in the mountains near Sumpter, Oregon. There was an inch of snow on the ground as I followed a dry creek bed uphill through a stand of second-growth timber. I watched the trail for elk sign and noticed fresh coyote tracks. The prints were so crisp that the edges hadn't started to crumble yet. The animal was apparently unaware of my presence behind him.

With growing interest I worked out his path: saw where he'd investigated old rabbit droppings and sniffed at porcupine tracks. I had to remind myself why I was there in the first place, and to watch the

Chris Lakey hunts coyotes in the desert. Gary Lewis photo.

sidehills and not the trail.

But the elk had made themselves scarce. When the trail ended in a box canyon, I looked again to see whether I was still behind the coyote. The tracks pointed up a timbered slope and the droppings he left— well, let's just say they still looked warm. I decided to make the most of my situation, sat down against a tree and took out my predator call.

After letting loose with a mournful wounded rabbit squall, I waited for a moment, listening and looking. After fifteen seconds I resumed calling, softer this time. Then I saw him!

He ran down the slope toward me, tongue hanging out. If there was a free meal happening, he wanted to know about it. But the moment I quit calling he put on the brakes. He hadn't spotted me yet but it was evident that he sensed something amiss.

I dropped the call and lifted my rifle. He was already running by the time I centered him in the scope, heading back the way he'd come. I tightened up on the trigger. *So what if I hadn't seen any elk?* 🌿

Coyotes aren't the only animals that will respond to a predator call. I've called in bear, deer, bobcat, ravens, and even a couple of hunters. It's exciting, and the memories generated make the hunt one to remember.

A fawn-in-distress or a dying-rabbit call costs only a few dollars and can be easily mastered. Not only is coyote hunting a lot of fun but it helps to reduce the predator population, which in turn reduces the number of deer and antelope fawns and elk calves that are lost to coyotes each year.

The first two hours in the day and the last two hours of light in the evening are the best times for calling. A coyote may respond any time of day but the likelihood is greater at first and last light.

The coyote knows that the sound of a rabbit in distress means an easy meal if it can take the rabbit away from whatever is killing it. That's why a dominant coyote will sometimes come right in, while a younger dog might hesitate.

Put fright and pain in your call. The first sounds a rabbit makes when captured are a series of squalls which then become gasping cries. If the predator shifts its grip then the squalls might come again. Keep in mind that a rabbit has little lung capacity. Calls should be a series of short cries.

Study the land and determine likely approaches a coyote might make. The wind is of utmost importance. Situate yourself downwind from where the coyote is likely to be. If you have partners, situate them up to 30 yards away from you as the caller. The predator will come right to *you*, so they should be close by.

Wear full camouflage and grease paint on hands and face. Keep all movement to a minimum. As coyotes approach they will be zeroed in on the location of the caller. Call in one location for at least fifteen minutes before moving on. Depending on the topography you might only need to move a quarter of a mile before calling again.

Set up to call coyotes from where the expected approach is clearly visible. Gary Lewis photo.

Some callers are now using confidence decoys to lure the coyotes in. There are jack rabbit decoys available that give the coyote something to look at as it approaches. Other hunters simply use an old stuffed animal that approximates the natural.

Coyotes perform the valuable function of keeping rodent and rabbit populations in check. However, coyote populations across the west have increased, and deer and antelope herds are suffering as coyotes take a large number of fawns.

Good places to watch for coyotes are where they find their principal foods. Fields, meadows, and prairies are full of mice; brushy draws hold rabbits and upland birds. Wherever there are plenty of antelope or deer, there will be coyotes close by. In the spring, when ungulates are giving birth to their young, a fawn-in-distress call can draw in predators. You might even bring in an angry deer.

When you find an area that has all the right coyote "foods," look for sign. Coyotes use trails and waterholes just like the other animals. If there are coyotes in the area you will see their sign. Coyote droppings are about the same size as a dog's, but the scat will be small and twisted on the end. It will contain undigested bits of whatever the animal has been feeding on. I have seen deer hair, bits of rabbit and mouse fur, and even berries in coyote droppings.

Coyotes also need a den to raise their pups in during the spring and summer, and for shelter in extreme conditions. A good coyote hunting area will be adjacent to food sources, but also give ample cover to hide from their enemies.

In September and October the young of that year are out searching for food on their own. The population is strongest at that time of the year and many coyotes lose their skins during deer and elk seasons. But the coyote pelt is best after the first snows and a tanned pelt or a coyote rug makes a fine trophy to remind you of a successful hunt.

Check regulations carefully before hunting predators outside your home state. Some Western states make predator hunting easy for the non-resident. Others require the purchase of additional licenses. Know before you go.

Chapter 16

MAKING EVERY SHOT COUNT

How well you sight in your rifle before the season has a big effect on the success your season will bring. Yet this truth is ignored by many hunters for the simple reason that they have never learned how to sight in a rifle scope.

I am amazed at the men I know who can run companies, tie trout flies on size 18 hooks, or rebuild a carburetor, yet are afraid to try a simple thing like sighting in their deer rifle.

Like anything else, you have to do it a few times to become comfortable. But don't go afield until your rifle and scope combination is proven to place five careful, bench-rested shots in, at least a three-inch circle when shot from a rest.

First, we'll talk about the scope itself. *How do you choose one from the bewildering array available?*

Narrow down your choices by deciding how much magnification you want. In a short-range rifle like a .30-30 or a .45-70, a two-power scope is a good choice. Shots will be at close range and the wide field of view afforded by the low power scope will allow the hunter to find the target quickly.

I like a fixed four-power scope on my .243 and my 7mm Magnum. The four-power is adequate for shots out to 300 yards. I try not to shoot at distances beyond that, though I can and have made those shots on deer-size game. The four-power is simple. With it, there is never the chance that the scope will be set on a higher magnification when the shot must be taken at close range.

The problem with using higher power in your scope is that it reduces the field of view. Field of view is the expanse of the subject within the field of the optical circle. As magnification is increased, the field of view diminishes. I have talked to many hunters who, when given a close-range opportunity, could not find the animal in the scope they had left dialed in at the maximum power. It's easier to find the target quickly in the scope when the field of view is larger.

Variable power scopes do have their place in deer hunting. For a gun that doubles as a varmint gun, a variable scope makes good sense. But I always recommend to my hunting partners that they leave the scope set at four- or five-power while deer hunting. For most big-game shooting out to 300 yards, a magnification in this range is sufficient.

Reticles vary from a simple post with an aiming dot to military style mil-dots, allowing the scope to be used as a range-finder. Plain crosshairs are fine but a duplex-style crosshair is my choice on a hunting scope because the outer portion of each crosshair is very thick, tapering to a thin, aiming intersection. This configuration allows your eye to go quickly to the center of the scope.

Consider light-gathering capability next. There are two tube diameters available for big game scopes. The one-inch (25mm) tubes are most common and 30mm tubes are growing in popularity thanks to European influence. Transmitted light reaches the eye better with wider internal lenses and a larger tube. But 5mm may not make enough of a difference to justify the higher cost of the larger tube.

The most important light gathering feature is the size of the objective lens. The cone of light projected from the rear of the scope should coincide with the diameter of your eye's pupil at low light. This is measured by arriving at the exit pupil. It should be between 5mm and 7mm. This is computed by dividing the objective diameter by the scope's magnification. So a 32mm objective with 4x magnification has an exit pupil of eight. A 40mm objective with 8x magnification has an exit pupil of five.

Be more concerned with lens quality than lens size. A good scope will have coated lenses. The coating reduces reflection and enhances the passage of light, improving the clarity of what the hunter can see through the scope.

Choose the scope that is best for the type of hunting you intend to use it for, and use quality rings and mounts to make it a part of your rifle.

Follow these steps in mounting the scope to your gun:

Fasten the mounts and rings to your rifle according to the manufacturer's directions, using a locking compound on the threads to keep the installation secure. Align the rings using a one-inch dowel.

Remove the tops of the rings and insert the scope, snugging the scope down—but not so tight that it won't turn in the rings. The next step is adjusting the eye relief.

Eye relief is critical because you need the proper distance between

Photo by Tiffany Lewis.

the lens and your eye to see the whole field of view without moving your head back and forth to find the right focus.

From a standing position, bring the rifle to your shoulder and find the natural spot for your cheek to rest on the stock. Push the scope as far forward as you can while still seeing the entire field of view from your cheekrest.

Raise the rifle to your shoulder a few times with your eyes closed, opening them when the stock is against your cheek. When you are satisfied with the position of the scope, tighten the rings a bit more, still allowing enough play to rotate the scope with your fingers. The next step is to adjust crosshair alignment to prevent canting.

The vertical wire in your scope should be perfectly vertical. Turn the scope in the rings until the vertical crosshair is straight up and down. Hold the rifle at arms length or set it in sandbags, backing off to check from a distance. When you are satisfied that the crosshairs are perfect, finish tightening the rings.

Focus the eyepiece by holding your gun to your shoulder and pointing at a blank wall. Bring the eyepiece up, check the reticle, adjust for focus, and do it again until the reticle is sharp and clear every time you bring the gun to your shoulder.

The first step in sighting-in your scope and rifle combination is bore-sighting. Do this at the shooting range. Remove the scope's windage and elevation caps. Remove the bolt from the gun and set the gun firmly in sandbags or a vise and then sight through the barrel at an object 100 yards away. Sight through the scope and make the adjustments to bring the crosshair in line with the object. Verify by looking again through the bore. Now your gun is bore-sighted. It is probably not accurate enough yet for deer hunting. Now you are ready to zero your rifle.

With a good rest from the shooting bench, fire two or three shots at your target. Examine the pattern and mark your shots on the paper. Every click of your 1/4 increment scope will move point of impact 1/4 at 100 yards. Fire another group of three shots and adjust again. I pattern my .243 to hit three inches above point of aim at 100 yards. This allows me to hold directly on the target, hitting point of aim at three hundred yards. At closer ranges my bullets may strike three inches high but it is still in the kill zone for coyotes, antelope or deer.

Sight your rifle for the longest useful range. And spend whatever time and ammunition it takes to learn how your rifle/scope/cartridge combination performs at different distances.

WHEN TO TAKE THE SHOT

Every situation and every deer is different. When your opportunity presents itself, you have to play the hand you're dealt. Or pass. Knowing when to shoot and when *not* to shoot are as important as sighting in—especially for bowhunters.

WHEN I HUNT DEER WITH A BOW, I am looking for relaxed deer. One year I hunted at the end of the pavement, about ten miles from town. My archery tag allowed me to take one buck with visible antler.

As the sun came up, I was sneaking into the wind along a hiking trail, well-hidden by tall manzanita. Parallel to my trail was a game trail about thirty yards over. I saw a narrow-racked three-point come even with me as I emerged from the manzanita.

He was still, his nose testing the air, tense—and he was just thirty yards away. I nocked an arrow, muffling the string snap against my shirt. At full draw, I settled the thirty-yard pin behind his shoulder and concentrated on a smooth release and follow-through.

I have never made a better shot! The arrow did just what it was supposed to. The deer didn't. At the sound of the string it crouched and sprang. By the time the arrow flashed through the space where the deer had been, the deer was in mid-leap. The broadhead passed harmlessly beneath the buck and stuck in the dirt. 🌿

Ear and tail positions tell a lot about the animal's tension. A deer whose ears are rotated forward is listening for danger. If he hears anything at all, he's gone. Wait until the animal flops his ears, relaxing, before you shoot.

Bowhunters should look for two types of shots: the broadside of a relaxed deer or the quartering-away shot. Picture the vitals as positioned just behind the shoulder and low on the body. Think three-dimensionally. The vitals are a ball inside of a box. To hit the ball you have to send that arrow or bullet into the box at an angle that will strike the ball.

When a deer or antelope is quartering away from you, the point of entry must start farther back on the deer's body. Your arrow or bullet may have to enter from behind the rib cage, traveling through the body cavity before destroying organs.

Watch the animal's reaction to your shot. What the deer does at impact will tell you how good your shot was and what you need to do next.

If the animal jumped at the shot, you probably shot too low. Check your arrow. You may find a few white belly hairs if you creased its belly. If hit in the paunch, a deer hunches up, drops his tail, and heads for cover. If there is blood, digested food, and quite a bit of hair on the arrow, the animal is hit low in the belly. Give it time to lie down and stiffen up. The deer won't run far if it isn't chased, though you might find it in the thickest cover.

If the animal dropped, you may have made a perfect shot, but don't go looking for the deer until you have nocked another arrow or chambered another round. If the antler was struck, the skull creased, or a vertebra nicked, the deer might just be unconscious. Be ready, your trophy could go bounding away while your partner slaps you on the back.

If there's no indication of a hit, investigate anyway. You owe it to the deer and to yourself. You may find hair at the site. Follow the tracks. More than once, I've followed up animals that I thought had escaped, only to find them piled up a hundred yards away.

Deer who are hit in the liver will leave dark blood on the trail. Do your best to find it. The deer will die in less than an hour.

Deer can be hit in the brisket or the fleshy parts of the legs and still survive. But every effort should be made to recover the animal. Sometimes there will be enough blood from those hits to allow the hunter to follow and get in position for another shot.

I HAVE SHOT TWO DEER at long range and one at short range that became difficult to find. I think the hardest to recover was the 70-yard shot I made on a blacktail.

(I always tie orange flagging at the spot I'm standing when I shoot. It is a practice I learned in bowhunting. It has saved me lots of time during rifle season, too.)

At my shot, the deer vanished. No retreating hoofbeats told me that I missed. Nothing moved except the tops of the willows in the wind. I tied my flagging to a bush and climbed down, headed to the spot where I thought I would find the deer. Nothing.

I spent the next twenty minutes slogging around in brush that was eight feet tall. The day was warm and I began to be concerned that the meat would sour while I fought my way around in the brush.

I laid my red plaid shirt on a bush where I believed I would have found the deer. Then I climbed back up to my orange ribbon. I looked at my shirt through the opening in the trees I'd shot the deer through. My shirt was twenty yards downhill from where I thought my deer should have been. I searched uphill and found my buck. 🦌

That's how to do it on short-range shots. At longer range, use your compass.

I WAS ON KODIAK ISLAND. The deer was standing across the canyon when I shot him. Through my binoculars, I studied the terrain, committing the surroundings to memory. It always looks different when you get over there.

I took a compass heading on the deer's position, turned the dial to orient myself to North and fixed the path to take.

I had to cross the deep snow of the canyon again, work my way up through the alders (keeping an eye out for brown bears) and out into the clearing where the buck lay. Night comes quickly in December. I moved fast.

I selected intermediate landmarks and worked my way to each one in succession, finally reaching the little clearing where the buck had been standing. Searching in ever-widening circles, I hit the blood trail and followed it down to my buck. 🦌

By paying attention to the deer's reaction to your shot, you will be able to put all the clues together to help you track down your trophy. By doing your part on the follow-up to the shot, you'll spend less time looking for downed game.

SLINGS

I picked up a well-used leather sling at a second-hand store. It seemed just the thing for my well-used Remington. It was to come in handy...

A sling can be simply a device used to carry a gun on a hunter's body or it can be much more. The sling I like is narrow, less than an inch wide. It rides easily between the shoulder and collarbone, not slipping off like the wider, padded slings sometimes do. Used correctly, it can also transform a person into a stable shooting platform.

Think about it. It's the moment the hunter has been waiting for. A mule deer buck appeares, seemingly out of nowhere. The hunter has dreamed of the moment for months. It is happening. Out of breath from climbing, adrenaline coursing in his veins, he lifts his rifle and tries to find the animal in the scope. He seeks to control his breathing, nerves, and twitching muscles long enough to make a steady shot without a rest.

A sling can help him do it. By wrapping his forearm once around the leather strap, he can steady the gun, putting pressure against shoulder and supporting arm to create a solid platform before the trigger squeeze.

ONE RAINY OCTOBER DAY, I made such a shot on a muley buck. To get the deer out of the woods, I found another use for the sling.

I thought I would drag the buck along the bluff and then find an easy way up the hill to the truck. But the trail cut sharply to the left and down. There was no other way to drag the deer but downhill to the creek. On the steep bank the deer tumbled and slid and there was nothing to do but go with it.

I was already wet from the pounding rain so I stepped into the creek and towed the deer through the pools and down the rapids toward the road. Then I saw the waterfall.

I was in a steep gorge with nothing but shale and high cliffs on either side. No way out. It was thirty feet to the water below and I didn't relish the thought of just letting the deer go over. There was a deep pool at the bottom but the rocks were jagged on either side. Without a rope, I risked damaging the meat and the antlers for which I had worked so hard.

I removed the sling from the gun and strapped it around the base of the antlers. Wedging my feet under a boulder to keep from going over with it, I lowered the animal over the cascade, letting go when I ran out of sling. The buck splashed into the pool below.

I picked my way down around the falls to the pool. I waded in and retrieved my buck and the sling—which was now twice as long as it had been when I started out that morning. 🦌

There *are* times when the hunter is better off without a sling. One might be on a horseback hunt where the rifle is stowed in a scabbard. A sling on a rifle carried in such a manner creates potential for an expensive mistake. If a branch happens to snag the sling, it can rip the rifle out of the scabbard as the horse passes by.

Other times it doesn't pay to have a rifle slung are while still-hunting or when taking part in a deer drive. A friend of mine does a bit of guiding. He tells his hunters to carry their rifles in their hands. In his method of hunting, the deer are running when they're spotted. The hunter whose rifle is slung over his shoulder is likely to bring up his gun too late, missing his best opportunity.

Don't hurry the shot. If possible, take a rest and take your time. Regular shooting practice during the off-season will pay off. Gary Lewis photo.

Another sling that provides a different approach to carrying a gun is called the Norris Body Sling. It is a system that you strap on top of your hunting clothes. The gun rests in two quick-release loops across your chest, muzzle pointed toward the sky. The manufacturer also recommends the sling for bowhunters and fishermen. The weight of the weapon is distributed across the torso rather than suspended from the neck. With nearly instant access, it could be the answer for the person who wants their hands free for climbing, paddling, or just eating a sandwich.

I used the Norris Body Sling on a duck hunt and was very satisfied.

While launching, beaching, or rowing the boat, the gun was strapped across my chest, out of the way. When the mallards jumped, framed in a spray of water against the reflected sunrise, the gun was instantly available, falling into my fingertips as I pressed the release buttons.

When I hunted black bear in Alaska I thought of another use for the body sling. A fisherman working his way up a salmon stream could carry a .30-30 or a short-barrel shotgun across his chest. If a salmon-feeding bear was encountered, the fisherman could become a bear hunter in the instant it took to drop the fly rod and press the release buttons on the body sling.

A rifle sling can become a liability if it is too heavy. Some hunters favor a sling that has loops for extra bullets. If the gun is shouldered for a quick shot and the sling is not wrapped around the forearm, the sling tends to wobble. A wobbling sling, weighted down with bullets or extra leather, can unbalance the crosshairs enough to make a bullet miss or wound.

Whether you pursue black bear, deer in the dark woods, or ducks from a dory, the sling of choice should be a carefully considered component of your hunting gear.

AMMUNITION AND ACCURACY

I BOUGHT MY REMINGTON 243 from a target shooter who had a matched set. The blued-barrel was matte-finished and the hardwood stock was plain; but when I brought the rifle to my shoulder, worked the bolt, eased the slack out of the trigger, and dropped the firing pin on a dummy round, I knew it was a gun that would serve me well.

I ordered a scope, set it in Leupold rings, bought two boxes of cartridges, and drove out to the range.

At 100 yards the factory-loaded ammunition printed a ragged five-shot, five-inch group. I opened the second box and fired five rounds of another company's ammunition. The second group was just as ragged, printing left, right, low, and high on the paper with little indication of any pattern.

After shooting the remaining cartridges I headed for the telephone.

It was time to call a handloader. My father-in-law was only too happy to finally prove what he'd been telling me for years.

First, we floated the barrel. A rifle's wooden stock expands and contracts with moisture, cold, and heat. When a bullet is fired from a rifle, the barrel vibrates like a tuning fork. When the barrel comes into contact with the stock, its barrel reacts to the pressure. The result is a variation in the down-range placement of the bullet. By floating the barrel, the gun-smith is able to make the rifle consistent by reducing the effect weather variability has on accuracy.

Bob Nosler (left) and John R. Nosler (right) with two fine whitetail bucks they took on a Texas cowboy hunt at Nail Ranch near Albany, Texas. Photo courtesy Bob Nosler.

Start by removing wood from the stock and then seal the barrel channel with a lacquer to reduce wood expansion/contraction. Next, build a fiber-glass platform in the stock on which the action will rest. This allows the barrel to be raised above the wooden channel. When the gun is fired, the barrel is free to vibrate consistently, shot after shot.

Second, we developed the optimum load for the rifle. I seated primers and my father-in-law, Paul, measured out powder, tipping the measure into a funnel, filling the cases with propellant. I watched as he made the measurements and adjustments, determining how the bullet would be seated in the case for best accuracy.

The first handloads through my rifle punched three little holes in the paper that I could cover with a quarter. Zeroing the scope took a few more shots, and by that time I was a believer in what loads tailored to my rifle could do for accuracy.

I changed loads a few years later, dropping from a 105-grain spitzer to a 95-grain Nosler bullet. Shooting from a rest, three shot groups with all the holes touching are not uncommon.

Handloaders now have more options than ever in their quest for accuracy. Many companies offer a black Molybdenum Disulfide coating on their bullets. Moly coatings reduce friction in the barrel and in flight, as well as allowing less build-up in the barrel. Shooters using the coating on their bullets are getting more speed and better accuracy.

RIFLE CALIBERS FOR DEER AND ANTELOPE

What is the right round for the deer and antelope hunter? There are a lot of theories on that subject. Some subscribe to the 'one size fits all' approach. Others want a different gun for each season. There are a lot of choices out there.

One of the most important things the hunter should take to the woods with him is his own practiced skill in shooting his chosen round. Many weapons are legal for deer and elk, but fewer can be considered the *right* choice in many situations.

The 223 Remington was developed for the military in the late 50s and early 60s. Bullet weights range from 40- to 70-grains and reach speeds up to 3800 feet per second. Bolt-action rifles provide the best accuracy for this economical, light-recoil round. The 223 Remington is an excellent choice for small game and coyotes out to 250 yards and beyond. Legal in many states for deer and antelope, it is a marginal round for any big-game animal because of the light weight of the bullet.

The 22-250 Remington was introduced as a commercial round in 1965.

Chelsea McLagan, and her father, Jon, with Chelsea's first mule deer. Best calibers for new hunters include the 243, 6mm Remington, 257 Roberts, and 7mm-08. Bullet choice and shot placement are critical. Photo courtesy Jon McLagan.

Using bullets in the 40- to 70-grain range, recoil is manageable and the rifle has a long reach of 300 yards or more. The 22-250 is an ideal round for coyote hunters who like to hunt rockchucks from time to time. It's an outstanding choice for varmints at long range, but not a good choice for deer or antelope.

For the hunter that wants varmint versatility in a big-game rifle, the 243 Winchester is hard to beat. Its flat trajectory makes it great for coyotes, javelina, antelope, and deer. Bullet weights range from 55- to 105-grains. Also, the 243 bullet is less affected by wind than the 22 centerfires and has more energy downrange.

The lightweight 243 Winchester is certainly not the rifle for all seasons, but a shooter can find a lot to like in the little cartridge. 55-grain polycarbonate-tipped projectiles can reach muzzle velocities of close to 4000 feet per second. And the heavier varmint bullets will buck the wind better than lighter 22 centerfires, while recoil is only slightly increased. Big game hunters enjoy more versatility because they can use a 95- or 100-grain round on deer in the fall and the same bullet on varmints during the rest of the year.

The 6mm Remington is another cartridge in the same class as the .243. Its longer case allows it to be loaded hotter than the .243. The difference in recoil is marginal.

In target, varmint, or big game shooting, bullet placement is the key. The easy recoil of the .243 or 6mm makes either round a great place to start for the beginner and a good place to stay for somebody who appreciates tack driving accuracy and versatility.

The .257 Roberts was introduced in 1934. For many years, pressures were limited by ammunition manufacturers to guard against blowing up older bolt-action rifles built on Model 93 and Model 95 Mauser actions. With low recoil and good accuracy potential, this caliber is an ideal all-around deer and antelope rifle when factory +P or hand-loaded ammunition is used. Best bullet weights for deer are between 100 and 120 grains.

The .25-06 Remington is an outstanding long-range deer and antelope caliber because of its ability to generate high velocities while maintaining good accuracy. Best bullet weights for deer-sized game are between 100 and 120 grains.

The .260 Remington was introduced in 1997. This medium-bore, mild-recoil round has the potential for great accuracy when loaded with 120-, 125-, and 140-grain bullets. Its only drawback is that if you run out of ammo in the middle of nowhere, the local hardware store is not likely to carry it. But if I were looking for a new deer rifle right now, that would be it—in Remington's Model 700 Titanium or their lightweight Model 7. I would top it with a Leupold scope and feed it 125-grain Nosler Partitions and use it for any deer hunt from South Dakota to South Carolina. The only place where I might feel under-gunned with this caliber would be on Kodiak Island. There a fellow might encounter something bigger than a blacktail deer with the ability to ruin a day with one sweep of a giant paw.

Outdoor writer Jack O'Connor was a longtime booster of the .270 Winchester for several reasons. Its recoil is mild, trajectory is relatively flat, and the bullet diameter is large enough to be effective on big game. The .270 consumes a diet of 130- to 160-grain bullets, perfect for deer-sized game. If your gun will double as an elk rifle, feed it 160-grain loads.

The 7mm-08 Remington is in the same class as the .270, albeit with slightly heavier bullets due to the increased diameter (.284). This is another ideal round for deer-sized game. Bullet weights run between 120 and 175 grains.

The 7mm Remington Magnum was introduced in 1962. Because of its versatility, it's one of the most popular rounds used throughout the West. It is suitable for all big game, from antelope to elk and black bear. I carried mine to Kodiak Island where I used it for Sitka blacktail. Bullet weights run between 120 and 175 grains. It's the caliber I use when I might be taking longer shots.

The .30-30 Winchester is the choice of many deer hunters, particularly in the coastal mountains and in the whitetail woods of the East. The first two deer rifles I owned were lever-action .30-30s. For the most part, they are reliable but not overly accurate beyond 150 yards. Use this gun when shots at game are not expected to exceed 100 yards. 150- to 170-grain bullets are optimum for this close-range deer gun.

The .308 Winchester is another caliber that is synonymous with versatility. Like the .270, 7mm Magnum, and .30-06, the .308 can be used to good effect on deer, antelope, elk, and medium-sized black bear. Its recoil is not punishing and its accuracy is legendary. The .308 is the round of choice for most police and military snipers. The best bullets for this caliber range between 150 and 200 grains.

The .30-06 Springfield may be the most common round used across the west for deer, elk, and bear. Bring a .30-06 to camp and few people will question your choice in a deer rifle. It is accurate and has plenty of knock-down power with good trajectory (as far as most hunters are capable of shooting). For deer and pronghorn, use a 150- to 180-grain bullet. If your rifle will go elk or bear hunting with you, consider using 200- or 220-grain loads.

You don't need any more power or bullet weight in a deer rifle, though many hunters use rounds like the .300 Winchester Magnum and .35 Whelen to good effect.

Spend time in the off-season shooting varmints or targets at the range. Learn where your gun shoots at different distances. The most important thing about picking a rifle to use in the pursuit of deer and antelope, is to choose a round you can shoot well and often.

Shooting regularly is the key to success. Whatever deer rifle you pick, buy its counterpart chambered for .22 rimfire. Whether you shoot a semi-auto, slide-action pump, lever-action, bolt gun or single shot, you can find a .22 rifle that will stand in for low-budget shooting practice.

If you have a scope on your deer rifle, also put one on your .22. Take it hunting for squirrels or rabbits. Learn to shoot it at moving and stationary targets, and practice at different distances. The goal is to train your eyes and hands to work quickly at acquiring the target and squeezing the trigger.

If rabbits or squirrels aren't plentiful where you live, have someone throw clay pigeons for you, using a hill for a backstop. Line up your sights and swing the muzzle so the front sight moves up to the streaking target and passes it to a spot just a little ahead. Squeeze off your shot while you are still swinging. Leading the target is necessary because the bullet takes time to reach the target.

Your lead will vary with the speed of the target and the range, but experience will teach you how much lead to use.

Spot-and-stalk tactics paid off for Bud Gabriel during archery season in North Central Oregon. His son, Luke, displays the dandy buck they took after a long sneak. Photo by Bud Gabriel.

Wild game meat is not only good tasting, it's good for you. The hunt is an expression of our freedom and heritage. Gary Lewis photo.

Chapter 17

AFTER THE SHOT

OUR HEADLIGHTS CUT LIKE KNIVES through the heavy fog. As the morning sun gave light to our cloud-shrouded world, we looked out on an abbreviated landscape of yellow grass and silver sage.

The gravel road was intersected by a dirt lane and a fence line. Turning onto the side road, little better than a cattle track, we followed the fence uphill through a stand of scattered junipers. The road ended at a cross fence where we parked and parted company, our whispered plans turning to vapor in the frozen air.

I watched my friend until he was swallowed by the swirling mists, then turned and pushed ahead, moving each time only as far as I could see, examining each new vista the fog afforded.

I had covered about 300 yards in this manner when I saw the deer. They had seen me first and I watched them trot into the fog and out of sight. I found their tracks and followed, spotting them again after a few minutes. Waiting for a clear shot, I chose my spot and took the slack out of the trigger, feeling the push of the rifle against my shoulder. A good supply of winter meat was assured. 🦌

Bullet placement is the first consideration in the care of your game. Properly placed, a good bullet will down the animal quickly with little meat damage. Taking the time to know your quarry's anatomy before you hunt will pay off when it's time to take the shot. Taking the time to choose your target carefully will mean that as little damage as possible is done to the meat.

An animal on the ground doesn't mean the hunt is over. In fact, the most critical phase of the process begins then. The animal should be cleaned within ten to fifteen minutes after it goes down. It doesn't have to be an unpleasant experience. A little preparation before the hunt goes a long way toward making that part easier. A novice should carry written, illustrated instructions to show the way.

In my pack I carry a knife, a bone saw, about 2 feet of cord, and surveyor's flagging to mark the trail back if I have to make more than one trip or go for help. In the truck I keep a tarp and deer bags to protect the meat.

Some people prefer to skin the animal in the field. That may be a good idea if you pack the meat out on your back. Let the conditions dictate how you'll handle it. On a warm day, you may need to remove the skin to allow the meat to cool faster. If dragging the carcass to the truck or camp, leave the skin on to protect it from the ground. When the meat is back in camp, skin and hang it in the shade, or double-bag it and let it cool in water.

On the road home or to the butcher's, there are a number of ways to keep the meat fresh. Displaying it on the hood of the truck is not one of them. Meat and heads tied on in such a manner are subject to spoilage by engine heat and exhaust and drying by the wind. And the practice is offensive to non-hunters. But don't hide it by piling luggage on top of the animal either, as that will insulate the meat against cooling. Allow for good movement of air and prop the cavity open to allow cool air to circulate. If you already started butchering it yourself, chances are you can get most of it into a cooler.

Wild game meat is not only good-tasting and good for you, it is an expression of our freedom and part of our heritage. Take the time before the hunt to decide how you'll care for the meat. Recognize how weather conditions and other factors play a part in spoilage. Wasting meat that could be saved is not only unethical, it's illegal. Properly cared for, deer and elk is some of the best tasting meat you can get. You owe it not only to the animal, but also to yourself, to take the best care of it you can.

INSTRUCTIONS FOR CLEANING DEER AND ANTELOPE

To clean a big game animal, you will need rubber gloves, (2) 18-inch lengths of cord, and a knife.

Place the animal on its back with the head uphill if possible.

Tie a cord around the penis to lessen the risk of urine tainting the meat.

Cut around the anus with your knife, then tie a cord around the end of the anus to keep excrement from the meat.

Cut from the pelvis bone up to the sternum, cutting around and laying aside the testicles (or the udder on a doe). Take care not to nick the intestines with the tip of the blade.

With the animal's head uphill, the internal organs will sag. Reach into the cavity and cut away the diaphragm, holding the stomach out of the way with your other hand.

Reach into the cavity and grasp the windpipe and gullet, pulling toward you. Cut them off as far forward as possible.

Tip the carcass so the internal organs slide out. You may have to cut some tissue that is holding the organs.

Turn the animal belly-side down to let the cavity drain.

Remove the legs below the knees and hang the carcass from the hocks.

Clean and sharpen your knife before skinning the animal.

PROPER FIELD CARE OF TROPHY HELPS TAXIDERMIST

The memory of your big game hunt can be preserved by taxidermy. Proper field care of your animal can contribute immensely to the quality of the finished trophy. Follow these rules after gutting the animal and cooling the meat:

Never make any cuts below the head, forward of the front legs. Do not cut the throat. Instead, skin down the back of the neck in a straight line, as near center as possible and then make a second cut forming a "Y" running to the base of the antlers. Cut carefully around the antlers and cut the skin away from the base.

Go slowly and carefully with the next two steps. Cut the ear cartilage from the bone on the inside and clean the meat away from the base of the ear. Skin along the skull, careful not to cut through at the eyelids.

Cut the lips close to the skull, leaving the lips attached to the skin. Make the cut inside the lips.

Leave enough of the cape for a shoulder mount. Cut inside the front legs in order to include the brisket for a complete shoulder mount.

The top portion of the skull, the antlers, and the bone between them, is all that is needed for mounting. Simply saw off the top of the skull through the center of the eyes after skinning is complete.

You will need approximately two pounds of non-iodized salt for a deer cape, approximately four pounds for an elk cape. Use your skinning knife to remove the extra meat from the hide and salt it heavily. Rub the salt into the scalp and leave it rolled up for a few hours in the shade. Then turn the skin flesh side out and salt it again. Roll it up and let it drain some more.

Take the hide and antlers to a taxidermist as soon as possible or put them in the freezer, wrapped in plastic.

Proper field care of your trophy will help your taxidermist do the very best job he can. The result will be a beautiful trophy of a hunt you will remember all your life.

EUROPEAN MOUNTS

If you want a unique trophy that you can prepare yourself, consider making a European mount of your buck deer.

For a European mount, peel the skin over the head and nose. If special care is taken, the cape can be saved and sold or traded to a taxidermist.

Wear rubber gloves and eye protection for the following work:

With a hacksaw or similar tool, cut into the cranium, aiming for a spot just below the eyes. Discard lower jaw.

With a small, sharp knife, trim out the brains and eyeballs. Cut the extra meat away from the skull and discard.

Outside, start water boiling in a big kettle and pour some salt into the water. Boil the skull, keeping the antlers out of the water. When the meat is thoroughly cooked, remove it from the water.

Clean all dirt from antlers with water and a light bristle brush.

Next, trim the cartilage out of the nasal passages and chip away the dried meat from the various orifices on the skull.

Boil the skull again after all the meat and cartilage has been cut away. When withdrawing it from the water, pull it out fast to keep the fats on the water's surface from adhering to the skull again. Spray the skull quickly with water from a garden hose.

Next, mix a cup of bleach with clean water in your kettle. Allow the skull to soak in the bleach for twenty minutes. Don't let antlers come into contact with bleach. Remove and spray clean with the garden hose.

Allow the skull to air dry. Depending on the humidity, this will take from two days to two weeks. When the skull is dry, spray antlers with clearcoat lacquer. Allow lacquer to dry overnight. Mask the antlers and spray cleaned, bleached skull with flat white paint and allow to cure overnight.

The skull can then be hung from a nail or affixed to a display board for a trophy that will give you pleasure for the hunt it reminds you of and the effort that you invested in it.

ABOUT CHRONIC WASTING DISEASE

A condition called Chronic Wasting Disease (CWD) is becoming a point of concern for medical scientists, wildlife biologists, hunters, and their families. It is part of a disease group of which scientists know little about, called transmissible spongiform encephalopathies. Mad Cow Disease is another member of this disease group.

A small number of deer and elk are dying of CWD. Public health officials are keeping a close eye on this because of the potential threat to the health of humans who consume infected meat.

Nobody is certain how the disease is transmitted from one animal to another, but Mad Cow Disease can be acquired by eating the infected nervous tissue of cows.

What is frightening to health officials is the fact that these diseases are so hard to kill. They cannot be destroyed by ultraviolet light, bleach, radiation, or cooking temperatures.

Confirmed cases of CWD have been reported in Canada, Colorado, Wyoming, Utah, New Mexico, Nebraska, South Dakota, Oklahoma, Montana, Wisconsin, and other eastern states. Many states have joined in a surveillance effort aimed at containing the disease.

An infected deer or elk can only be diagnosed after it has died; that is why (in pen-raised herds of deer and elk) if one animal is found to be infected, to be safe all must be killed.

The Center for Disease Control and Prevention recently completed research that suggests there is little risk of the

Katie Coil with her Wyoming buck. Photo courtesy Paul Coil.

disease being transmitted to humans from the flesh of a deer or an elk. Still, health officials recommend a cautious approach.

Don't harvest an animal that appears sick or listless. Symptoms of CWD are weight loss, constant salivation, thirst, excessive urination, difficulty in swallowing, constant walking, and lowering of the head.

When field-dressing an animal from a region where CWD has been found, wear rubber gloves. Boning meat in the field is recommended. Avoid contact with the spinal cord and brain. Do not handle or consume the head, spine, eyeballs, spleen, or lymph nodes. Do not saw through the vertebrae. Do not saw through the skull to remove the antlers.

If it is necessary to saw through vertebrae or skull, it should be done last to avoid infecting meat with a tainted blade.

If you are hunting in an area where incidences of CWD have been reported (such as southeastern Wyoming or northeastern Colorado), you can submit the head of a harvested deer or elk to Wyoming State's Veterinary Laboratory (307-742-6638) or Colorado State University's Diagnostic Laboratory (970-491-1281). Freeze the meat, but do not eat it until the animal has been tested and found negative for CWD. Do not eat the meat of any animal that tests positive for CWD.

To date, there is no evidence pointing to the transmission of CWD to humans. Yet so little is known, caution is the best approach.

ABOUT LYME DISEASE

Cases of Lyme Disease have surfaced throughout the country. So far, the best defense seems to lie in being informed.

The disease was first diagnosed in 1977 at Yale University when doctors first called it Lyme Arthritis, naming the condition after the Connecticut town where it was first identified. Five years later, the bacterium that causes it (Borrelia burgdorferi) was discovered.

Lyme Disease is carried by the deer tick. It is delivered when the tick drinks a person's blood. The process takes more than 24 hours. Examination for ticks should be made at the end of each day spent in deer country.

Once the bacteria are in the body, they are carried through the skin, blood, and lymphatic fluid.

The first symptom of the disease is often a bulls-eye rash with an opening at the center. Recurring rash, fever, fatigue, aches in neck, head, muscles and joints are early symptoms that can point to Lyme. If not treated, the condition of the victim deteriorates. Ulcers, heart murmurs, deteriorating joints, internal infections, and constant fatigue await the undiagnosed and untreated.

Though Lyme has been reported throughout the country, some areas report higher incidence of the disease. Where temperatures are moderate, ticks thrive. In colder climates, where many ticks don't survive the winter, occurrence of Lyme in humans is minimal.

Lyme disease is not the only disease potentially carried by ticks. When dressing game, wear rubber gloves. Examine your clothing and body for ticks at the end of the day. If bitten by a tick, see a doctor for preliminary treatment. Know the symptoms of the disease. It is easily treated in the early stages, so see the doctor before the condition worsens. The disease is still so rare that hunters should not be worried—just informed.

David Salciciolli with his first buck. Photo courtesy Diana Salciciolli.

Chapter 18

THE FUTURE
OF DEER HUNTING

I encourage hunters to make every effort to involve their family and friends on at least one hunt per year.

When my oldest daughter was ten, I took her along on a hunt for mule deer in Eastern Oregon. She had passed hunter safety when she was eight and taken several rabbits with her 410 shotgun, but she had never been on a deer hunt where an actual deer was harvested.

We spotted a herd of seven deer from the road and planned our stalk. A dry creek bed allowed us to make our approach. We slid beneath a barbed wire fence and dropped down into the creek bottom. The wind howled down the valley out of the east. It swirled in the creek bed, sometimes in our faces, sometimes at our backs. We would have to move quickly to reach the deer before our scent did.

Tiffany followed, ten paces behind, as we moved along the rocky bed. I stopped to look back and saw the excitement in her eyes. She was enjoying this as much as I was. At the bend in the creek, we stopped. We were close. 50 yards away. I found a deer trail leading up out of the creek and followed it. The deer were still there. Six bucks, one doe.

I made sure of my target and squeezed the trigger, making an easy 40-yard shot.

Afterwards, Tiffany said she thought her heart would jump out of her chest. I knew just how she felt.

In the morning, we started for home, stopping to fish the John Day and the Deschutes Rivers. A steelhead grabbed my spinner, shook his head and was gone, leaving me breathless. As we headed back down the trail to the truck, we talked about the deer we had seen and the fish we didn't catch.

Tiffany will soon carry a rifle in deer season. Then *I* will follow *her* as she closes in on a deer, and I will try to keep the pounding of my heart from spooking the herd.

Of all the fringe benefits of spending time in the outdoors, the bonds we forge with family and friends are the most rewarding.

The End

Guy and Guy Schoenborn Jr. with a 4-point black-tail buck Guy Jr. took during a special youth hunt in Oregon's Santiam Unit.
Photo courtesy Guy Schoenborn.

Author and daughter on a recent hunt. Gary Lewis photo.

Time spent with family sweetens the outdoor experience. Target practice builds memories and skills as it prepares your child for further adventures. Gary Lewis photo.

CARPACCIO

Recipe courtesy Ed "Big Lunch" Hagen of Shepp Ranch, Idaho

Deer tenderloin	2 tsp Capers
1/2 each Balsamic Vinegar and Olive Oil	Juice of Lemon, Lime, or Orange
6-8 cloves Garlic	

Slice meat in thin, 2-inch strips. Prepare a marinade of Balsamic Vinegar and Olive Oil. Add in Garlic cloves, capers, and the juice of one Lemon, Lime, or Orange. Chill and marinate meat 4-6 hours. Drain marinade. Serve with crackers.

For me, camp cooking will never be the same after
spending a week at elk camp with Shepp Ranch in Idaho's
Gospel Hump Wilderness. On the fifth day, Ed shot a nice 4-point.
That night he served Carpaccio, made from the tenderloin.
—Gary Lewis

BRAUN'S DEER BURGER CHILI

Recipe courtesy Sheila Braun

1-16 oz. can drained Black beans	1 clove Garlic
1-16 oz. can drained Kidney beans	2 tsp Chili powder
2-14.5 oz. cans stewed Tomatoes	1 tsp Pepper
1/2 lb. browned deer Burger	1 tsp Cumin
1/2 cup chopped Onion	Salt to taste

If substituting dry beans, completely soften as directed on bag. Put all ingredients in crock pot in order listed. Stir occasionally. Cover and cook on Low for 10-12 hours. (High 5-6 hours) If you don't have a crock pot, simmer on stove 50 minutes to 3 hours.

Such a simple recipe, and so good.
Serve with cornbread and a green salad. Enjoy!
—Gary Lewis

Appendix

ADDRESSES OF STATE AGENCIES

Alaska:

Department of Game and Fish, PO Box 3-2000, Juneau, AK 99802-2000

Alberta:

Energy and Natural Resources Fish and Wildlife Division, Main Floor, North Tower, Petroleum Plaza, 9945-108 Street, Edmonton, AB T5K 2C6; (403) 427-6750.

Arizona:

Game and Fish Department, 2222 W. Greenway Road, Phoenix, AZ 85023; (602) 942-3000; website: www.azgfd.com.

British Columbia:

British Columbia Ministry of Environment, Wildlife Branch, Parliament Building, Victoria, BC V8V 1X5, Canada.

California:

Department of Fish and Game, 1416 9th Street, Sacramento, CA 95814; (916) 227-2244.

Colorado:

Division of Wildlife, 6060 Broadway, Denver, CO 80216; (303) 825-1192.

Hawaii:

Division of Forestry and Wildlife, 1151 Punchbowl Street, Room 325, Honolulu, HI 96813; Recorded Information (808) 522-8233, Office (808) 587-0166.

Idaho:

Fish and Game Department, 600 S. Walnut, PO Box 25, Boise, ID 83707; (208) 334-3700.

Montana:

Department of Fish, Wildlife and Parks, 1420 E. Sixth, Helena, MT 59601; (406) 449-2535.

Nevada:

Nevada Division of Wildlife, 1100 Valley Road, Reno NV 89512; (775) 688-1500.

New Mexico:

Game and Fish Department, #1 Wildlife Way, Santa Fe, NM 87505; (800) 862-9310, (505) 827-2923, (505) 476-8000; website: www.gmfsh.state.nm.us.

Oregon:

Oregon Department of Fish and Wildlife, PO Box 59, Portland, OR 92707; (503) 229-5403.

Texas:

Texas Parks and Wildlife, 4200 Smith School Road, Austin TX 78744; (800) 792-1112.

Utah:

Division of Wildlife Resources, 1596 WN Temple, Salt Lake City, UT 84116; (801) 538-4700.

Washington:

Game Department, 600 N. Capitol Way, Olympia, WA 98501-1091; (360) 902-2200.

Wyoming:

Wyoming Game and Fish Department, 5400 Bishop Blvd., Cheyenne, WY 82006-0001; (307) 777-4600.

---

*For your copy of *Blacktail Trophy Tactics II,* send $24.95 +3.50 s/h, c/o Grassroots Publications Dept. WDH, 1872 Willamette Street, Eugene, OR 97401